P9-DCD-377

100GardenTips
and Timesavers

By Walter Chandoha

Janet Marinelli
SERIES EDITOR

Sigrun Wolff Saphire
SENIOR EDITOR

Gerry Moore
SCIENCE EDITOR

Leah Kalotay
ART DIRECTOR

Joni Blackburn
COPY EDITOR

Steven Clemants
VICE-PRESIDENT,
SCIENCE &
PUBLICATIONS

Judith D. Zuk
PRESIDENT

Elizabeth Scholtz
DIRECTOR
EMERITUS

Handbook #182

Copyright © 2005 by Brooklyn Botanic Garden, Inc.

All-Region Guides, formerly *21st-Century Gardening
Series,* are published three times a year at
1000 Washington Ave., Brooklyn, NY 11225.

Subscription included in Brooklyn Botanic Garden
subscriber membership dues ($35 per year;
$45 outside the United States).

ISBN # 1-889538-69-8

Printed by Science Press, a division of the Mack
Printing Group. Printed on recycled paper.

**By using your common sense and a little ingenuity, you can not only save time and effort in the
garden but valuable natural resources too.**

100 Garden Tips and Timesavers

Improving the Soil

Pest Controls

Propagation

Garden Design

Container Gardening

Gardening Indoors

Vegetables

Trash to Treasure

Index and Contributors

Introduction

Gardeners share a universal problem—we don't have enough time. There simply are not enough hours in the day for our many projects: sowing, transplanting, and dividing plants; designing, building, and renovating gardens—not to mention the constant chores of weeding, pruning, and composting. There are regions of North America that allow gardening almost year-round, but most of us have

just six to eight months in which to fit everything from spring planting to fall harvest cleanup. And that's in between pursuing our careers and everything else we like to do during the summer, like swimming, golfing, visiting friends, and traveling!

In my more than 40 years of dirty jeans, calloused hands, and learn-as-I-go gardening on my 46-acre farm in northwestern New Jersey, I have planted many gardens with flowers, vegetables, fruits, herbs, and ornamental grasses. I've tried to make the most of my time in the garden by using a combination of inspira-

To get the most from my garden, I endlessly experiment with techniques such as succession planting.

As part of an ongoing project, I have been photographing my gardens from the same vantage points over each of the four seasons of the year.

tion, ingenuity, and a fair amount of common sense to find shortcuts to a beautiful, healthy, abundant garden.

Among the nine chapters in this handbook are "Gardening Techniques," "Improving the Soil," "Pest Controls," "Propagation," and "Vegetables," which include tips and techniques I've used over the years to protect and enhance the soil, save time and effort in watering, and extend the blooming or growing seasons of my flowers and vegetables.

As part of my career as a nature photographer, I've experimented with garden designs to achieve exciting color, texture, and composition in borders and container gardens throughout the seasons. The tips in "Garden Design" and "Container Gardening" will help you plan and create your own garden environments. In "Gardening Indoors" are ways to expand the space and season limits of your garden by growing plants indoors, as well as methods for preserving flowers and herbs for enjoyment year-round.

Finally, in "Trash to Treasures," I have applied my tendency toward frugality—something that seems to come naturally to gardeners—to think of ways to reuse materials on hand. None of the tips in this handbook call for materials fancier than cement blocks or wooden boards, and many call for recycling household "junk" like plastic jugs or items that have outlived their original use. For example, it dawned on me that my old golf bag and cart—fallen into disuse as my passion for gardening overtook my love of golf—would make a great carrier for long-handled tools. Not only does it work well in its new capacity but I've saved three or four cubic feet of landfill space.

100 Garden Tips and Timesavers has color-coded chapter bars for quick reference to general topics like gardening techniques and vegetables, and each tip is described with step-by-step instructions. Keep it handy for inspiration—it can even go with you to the garden, perhaps nestled in your golf-bag tool carrier!

Gardening Techniques

1 Deadheading Annuals for Repeat Blooms

To keep annuals blooming prolifically, remove their flowers immediately after they have peaked. Known as deadheading, this practice stops the flowers from forming seeds, spurring the plant to form more flower buds to take their place.

HOW TO DO IT

• Be vigilant—the more frequently you deadhead, the more profuse the blooms. A weekly stroll among the flower beds pinching back or clipping off spent flowers will also keep the garden looking fresh and tidy.

• Depending on the thickness and toughness of the flower's stem, use your fingers to pinch off dead blooms or clip them off with your pruner.

• Toward the end of the season, allow the final blooms of sunflowers (*Helianthus*), strawflower (*Bracteantha*

As long as spent blooms are not allowed to set seed, annuals will continue to flower until frost.

bracteata), and globe amaranth (*Gomphrena globosa*), as well as perennials like coneflowers (*Echinacea*) and astilbes, to remain on their stems to attract seed-eating birds and create winter interest in the garden.

• Collect the spent flower heads as you go to keep beds neat and help prevent

unwanted reseeding and invasiveness. If you want to save seeds for next season, allow a few of the best flowers to remain on the plant to ripen their seeds (see Tip #3).

(see Tip #3).

2 Pinching for Compact Plants

Many annuals and perennials are vigorous growers that tend to get leggy if allowed to grow unchecked. Pinching is a good way to foster bushy plants that produce lots of flowers.

HOW TO DO IT

• Seedlings displayed at nurseries in the spring are often already in flower—this is not only to show their color but also to induce us to buy them. If you sacrifice those first blossoms by pinching them out before planting, new stems will emerge from below

the pinch to make for fuller and more flowery plants later.

• For floriferous phlox with a longer bloom time, cut back a third of the stems of each clump when they're about a foot high. The uncut stems bloom first, and by the time they begin to wane, those that were cut back have produced multiple stems full of buds.

• Cut back tall sedums by three to five inches for bushy, thick-blooming plants.

• For plump domes of fall color, chrysanthemums must be pinched back early and often. When the seedling is a single stem with several sets of leaves, pinch away half of it. Incipient buds below the pinch will come to life and new stems will emerge. When they have grown to six to eight inches, pinch them back by half. Continue pinching until the end of July. As the days get shorter, buds will begin to cover the now nicely rounded mum. Even if you don't get around to pinching it back until June, there is still time to save it. Shear the leggy plant back to about ten inches or so. By the fall it will have filled out sufficiently to look presentable.

• Cut back asters periodically early in the season to avoid tall, floppy plants.

3 Saving Seeds of Annual Flowers

Even with diligent pinching and deadheading, the bloom season for annuals

Pinching back chrysanthemums early and often will produce dense domes of fall color.

Disbudding for Bigger Blooms

Getting lots of flowers through pinching back and deadheading sometimes means smaller flowers or ones with short stems. If what you really want are showier blooms suited for cutting, try disbudding. Pinch out tiny developing flower buds below a terminal flower bud to make that top bud produce a bigger flower. Many dahlias make buds at every leaf node, every eight to ten inches inches. For cut-flower bouquets, the stems may be too short for the size of the blooms. Pinching out several buds will produce stems that are better balanced. Some of the huge mums with five-inch-wide flowers that you see at florists are the result of disbudding: Large chrysanthemum plants are trained to only a few stems, and any buds that emerge below the top bud on a stem are pinched out. Disbudding minimizes the number of blossoms but maximizes the size of those remaining.

will eventually end. But after those beautiful flowers fade, their ripened seeds can be harvested for a free source of next year's blooms.

HOW TO DO IT

• Toward the end of the growing season, stop deadheading annuals (see Tip #1) to allow sufficient time for the seeds to ripen.

• To improve seed selection, pick two or three exceptional flowers—perhaps ones bigger then the others or with more intense colors—tie a piece of ribbon around the stems, and allow only these flowers to go to seed.

• When the flowers are completely mature and dry, snip them off the plant, gather the seeds, and store them in labeled bags in a cool, dry place.

4 The Benefits of Raised Beds

Whether simple soil plateaus or more elaborate structures made of planks, timber, cement blocks, or stone, raised beds of amended soil allow you to grow better and bigger ornamentals and vegetables that might not otherwise thrive, especially if you have heavy clay or very sandy soil. Raised beds also save water and fertilizer, which go only on the beds, not the adjacent walkways. Another advantage of raised beds is that culinary herbs and vegetables stay cleaner when grown off the ground.

HOW TO DO IT

• To build soil plateaus: In a flat garden, mound up soil from either side of what will later be walkways. Blend in compost and perhaps some organic fertilizer and rake the beds into ten-inch-high plateaus of any length and up to four feet wide. At four feet wide, the beds are accessible from either side.

• For an enclosed raised bed, select a site and rake it flat, then frame it with boards or timber or build a low wall of stones or cement blocks. After the enclosure is in place, fill it with compost and plant.

In addition to being practical, raised beds can add architectural dimension and texture to gardens.

- It's easy to modify the soil in raised beds to suit the plants or crops grown in each area. For example, add sand and additional compost to make a loose friable soil for carrots or spring-flowering bulbs; add lime to the bed for growing beets.

- Prepare raised beds in fall for early-spring planting. The elevated soil thaws out earlier and can be planted sooner than the rest of the garden, giving you an edge.

Soil Analysis Tells All

A couple of months before you plant, send soil samples to your local cooperative extension for a report on the type and level of nutrients in your soil as well as its pH level. It can also suggest ways to balance and improve the soil, such as adding lime.

5 | Extend the Season With Cold Frames

Cold frames are an ingenious way for cold-climate gardeners to eke out several extra weeks of gardening each spring and fall. Use them to give seedlings of vegetables and annuals a head start, overwinter hardy bulbs for an early flower show (see also Tip #23), harden off tender plants in spring, and keep vegetables in production deep into fall.

HOW TO DO IT

- Using cement blocks or boards, build a four-sided structure in a place that

A cold frame—easily constructed from materials you have on hand, such as boards and old glass-paned windows or doors—can give you a head start in spring and extend the fall harvest.

gets sun all day. Stack the blocks or boards higher on the north-facing side so that the frame slopes to the south. Make it as wide and long as your cover, which can be old storm windows or a glass-paned door.

• Place hay bales around the cold frame during the coldest months for extra insulation.

6 A Moss Carpet for Shade

How would you like a lawn that requires no mowing, no liming, no fertilizing, and recovers from a drought in two days? Shady, moist areas that usually constitute "problem" spots can be perfect for growing a moss lawn. If your grass is struggling in such an area, moss is most

A Winter Microclimate

To extend the season of my Zone 6 garden, I dug out the soil in my cold frame and replaced it with a deep layer of compost before putting the cement blocks in place. The wind-blocking, sunlit glass panes of the cover and the thermal mass of the blocks kept the interior favorable for growing salad greens from late fall to spring. In midwinter some of the greens froze, but the escarole and arugula survived and resumed growth in the spring.

Nurturing moss in a woodland garden avoids many of the headaches of growing grass in the shade.

likely already growing there—all you have to do is nurture it.

HOW TO DO IT

- Stop fertilizing and liming the soil for a year or so and let the grass die a natural death; moss will start to fill in the area.

- Nurturing a moss garden does take patience, but one way of hastening the process is to place fist-size plugs of moss on bare soil that's been slightly scraped, sprinkled with peat moss, and moistened with water.

- Hand pull any straggling grass blades and weeds. Use your bare hands or thin medical gloves—you'll need to get down between the patches of moss to pull the plant out by its roots, and with bulky garden gloves it's easy to pull up clumps of moss along with the weed.

- Avoid using treated tap water on your moss lawn; instead, collect rainwater (see Tip #15) or use nonchlorinated well water.

7 | Keeping a Moss Lawn Tidy

Moss makes a great alternative lawn when nurtured in shady, acidic spots where grass and other plants have a hard time thriving. But it doesn't like being raked come autumn's leaf fall.

For a low-maintenance hedge, look for shrubs such as forsythia, which has a graceful natural habit and requires little pruning.

Here are some ways to get rid of leaves without gouging your moss.

HOW TO DO IT

• Use a leaf blower to consolidate the leaves into a pile. They can either be gathered up by the armful or sucked up and shredded by a mulching mower with an attached leaf bag. The ground-hugging moss is untouched by the mower blades.

• In early fall, just as the leaves begin to drop, cover the moss with black plastic mesh, such as bird netting. Once a week or so, carefully gather up the mesh and remove the collected leaves for shredding and adding to the compost pile. Repeat this procedure until all the leaves have fallen from the trees.

8 Low-Maintenance Hedges

Not all hedges require heavy pruning. Flowering shrubs are especially good candidates for low-maintenance, informal living fences. They also provide color and sometimes fragrance, as well

as food and shelter for wildlife—all with minimal help from the gardener.

HOW TO DO IT

• Great shrubs for low-maintenance hedges include serviceberries (*Amelanchier*), forsythia, lilacs (*Syringa*), mock oranges (*Philadelphus*), shrub roses, flowering quinces (*Chaenomeles*), weigelas, azaleas, rhododendrons, viburnums, hydrangeas, and beautyberries (*Callicarpa*).

• American holly (*Ilex opaca*) produces bright berries in fall, but some culti-

Letting Go

Several years ago I planted a curved row of forsythias on a slope above my driveway with the thought of pruning it into the classic flattened pyramid. With regular pruning, by the second year after planting, I had the makings of a true hedge. But when the plants bloomed in the spring of the third year, they were so impressive as they fanned up from the ground I realized it would be a mistake to prune them into a formal hedge. Now, after two more years of growth, they have made me appreciate even more the natural aesthetics of an unpruned hedge. And they're so much less work!

This pyramid-shaped privet hedge sheds snow and allows sunlight and rain to reach all the branches.

vars eventually grow nearly tree size if left unpruned. The flashiest berry-producing shrub is winterberry (*Ilex verticillata*), which is deciduous and grows in Zones 3 to 9. Another red-berry producer is Yaupon holly (*Ilex vomitoria*), this one prefers more heat and is good from Zone 7 and warmer. All these hollies need both males and females growing near each other if berries are desired.

• Evergreens such as boxwood (*Buxus*), yews (*Taxus*), and arborvitaes are often sheared, but they are also very attractive if left to grow naturally. And untrimmed they have a big advantage over those that are severely pruned—they require far less work.

9 Pruning for Proper Hedge Shape

Formally pruned hedges should be wider at the bottom than at the top. This shape allows light and sun to reach all the way to the lower branches fostering their growth. In cold climates, this also prevents damage from excess snow accumulation that can disfigure the hedge and even break branches.

HOW TO DO IT

• When starting a new formal hedge with young nursery-bought plants, set them out according to the nursery instructions and prune them to six inches. Mulch with an organic mulch, and if there is no rain, water weekly. As new growth reaches eight to ten

Getting Even

To prune a level flattop pyramid, stretch a line tied between two sticks along the length of the hedge, make sure the height from string to ground is equal at both ends of the string, then trim the hedge just above the string. After the top is trimmed, work down the sides to the bottom, making sure to maintain a trapezoidal shape that is wider at the bottom than at the top.

inches, keep pruning it back by half to encourage fullness.

• Once the hedge reaches its desired height, you have several shape options: a flattened pyramid, the most popular form; a rounded top, which is good for less formal gardens, is not as vulnerable to snow damage, and also requires less work; or a topiary shape of your choosing. The important thing is to keep the hedge pruned wider at the bottom and tapering toward the top.

10 When to Prune Flowering Shrubs

Picking the right time to prune is key to healthy and attractive flowering shrubs.

HOW TO DO IT

• If a shrub blooms early in the spring on branches that formed the previous year, do all your pruning immediately after blooming. Early-blooming shrubs include forsythias, kerrias, mock oranges (*Philadelphus*), and lilacs (*Syringa*).

Wait until spring-flowering shrubs, such as kerrias and lilacs, are done blooming before pruning.

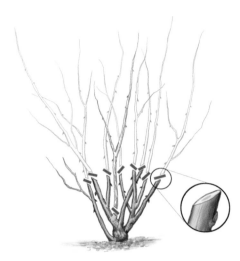

Remove dead canes and prune to ten inches high, cutting at a 45-degree angle above an outward-facing bud.

Prune out all canes below the graft union, as well as all but three or four of the strongest ones growing above.

Cut blooms for bouquets just above the first five-leaf cluster on the stem below.

- If the shrub blooms in late spring or in summer on new branches grown this season, prune in late winter or very early spring. Examples of late-blooming shrubs are rose of Sharon (*Hibiscus syriacus*), roses, and gardenias.

- Encourage more vigorous flowering of lilacs the following season by pruning off the seed heads that form after the flowers wane.

11 Pruning Hybrid Tea Roses

Many gardeners agonize about when to prune their hybrid tea roses. A handy rule of thumb is early spring, just about when forsythias begin to bloom. No forsythias around? When the leaf buds of the rose start to swell, it's time to prune.

HOW TO DO IT

- For more comfort and dexterity, keep your pruner hand bare and wear a thick leather work glove on the other to hold the prickly rose canes.

- Before pruning live canes, cut out dead ones—they'll be black, brown, or mottled instead of the vibrant olive-green of live canes.

- Prune out inward-pointing and crossing canes and remove weak and damaged canes.

- After removing dead wood, prune back live canes to about ten inches high. To train canes outward, away from the center of the rosebush, cut each one about a quarter of an inch above an outward-facing bud at a 45-degree angle.

- Rake up and dispose of all the pruned-out canes. Then remove the mound of protective mulch that you heaped around the bush in the fall after the soil froze. Use a gentle stream from the garden hose to wash away the compost mulch.

- With the mulch out of the way, check for canes emerging from below the swollen graft union and prune them out. Nonhybrid suckers that sprout from the rootstock can soon dominate the entire plant, and you don't want that 'Peace' rose to turn into a multiflora!

- Step back and look at your handiwork. Try to visualize how the rose will look when it is fully leafed out and blooming and ask yourself if it looks balanced. Now go back to the rose and prune out all but three or four of the thickest, strongest canes. Remember, strive for balance.

- Later in the season, as you cut roses for indoor bouquets or when you deadhead spent roses, make the cut just above the first five-leaf cluster lower down on the stem.

12 Rejuvenating Flowering Shrubs

Regardless of their time of bloom, if flowering shrubs have not been pruned for many years, are overgrown, have thick trunklike stems, and look ugly, drastic surgery may be advisable.

HOW TO DO IT

- Do heavy pruning in late winter before the buds swell.

- Don't do the whole job at once. Instead, spread the pruning task out over several years, removing no more than 20 percent of live wood in one year.

Rejuvenating an Old Hedge

A drastic solution for a misshapen, overgrown hedge is pruning it down to six inches above the ground—preferably in the spring. New growth will emerge from the stumps. When the new spaghetti-thin branches reach eight to ten inches, prune them back to five inches. New growth will emerge from the leaf nodes, and where you had one branch there now could be a half dozen or more. The following year repeat the procedure, cutting back half of the new growth. By the third year, the hedge will have grown tall enough to trim to the desired shape (see Tip #9).

Some older hedges could use some regeneration but not the severe pruning described above. Cut these hedges back by no more than a third for three years in a row. Yews (*Taxus*), hemlocks (*Tsuga*), arborvitae, boxwoods (*Buxus*), and Japanese holly (*Ilex crenata*) will all put forth new growth when pruned back, as will azaleas (*Rhododendron*) and forsythias. However, both azaleas and forsythias are more attractive when only lightly pruned (see Tip #8).

When rejuvenating an overgrown shrub, remove no more than 20 percent of live wood per year.

Encourage fresh branching by cutting back large old branches to six to eight inches high.

Over time, remove crossing branches and trim back new growth to promote a pleasing structure.

• Cut large branches that you want to eliminate six to eight inches above the ground. Dormant, incipient buds below the cut will come to life and you'll shortly have new growth. Note, however, that lilacs (*Syringa*) will produce a profusion of suckers and should be pruned level with the ground.

• Give the new branches a season to elongate, then prune them back by a third to encourage branching.

• In the following years, prune as needed to maintain good structure. Remove dead and broken branches and also continue to remove old wood if necessary.

13 Take Advantage of Microclimates

Every garden has spots that are just a little warmer or cooler than the surrounding area. The trick is to identify those places and use them to grow plants that otherwise might not thrive in your garden.

HOW TO DO IT

• Take a look at all built structures. The walls of a house or shed absorb the sun's heat during the day and release it during the night, creating a warmer microclimate. A south-facing wall is especially effective at retaining heat.

• Identify areas that are sheltered from cold, desiccating winds. A fence or a windbreak of shrubs or trees influences the climate in your garden: Placed in the path of prevailing winds, such a barrier blunts the force of the

Conifers planted west of this garden protect plants from prevailing winds and attract beneficial birds.

wind and just might make the difference between a borderline plant's surviving in a cooler zone or perishing.

• Conifers used as a windbreak have the added benefits of attracting beneficial birds (see Tip #32) as well as trapping heat, making the area adjacent to them somewhat warmer than other parts of the garden. Bodies of water do the same thing—they cool more slowly than air and keep the ground near the water just a bit warmer than soil farther away.

• Cooler spots come in handy as well, especially for vegetables like salad greens. Lettuce languishes in midsummer gardens, where the heat makes it wilt, turns it bitter, and causes it to bolt. To extend your harvest into the dog days, plant lettuce in the shelter of a corn row or along the shady side of a fence and mist it every day.

Create a Mini Microclimate

To give a boost to tender plants vulnerable in your climate, surround them with a stone or brick mulch—it will absorb the sun's heat during the day and release it slowly at night. To offer even more heat to the plants, create a "thermal mass" to soak up even more of the sun's warmth: Fill four or five plastic gallon-size milk jugs with water and set them atop the stone mulch.

Growing drought-tolerant plants, such as 'Bright Star' purple coneflower and black-eyed Susans, for late-summer color in the garden conserves resources and cuts down on watering chores.

14 Grow Drought-Tolerant Plants

Growing drought-tolerant plants in your garden increases your chances of a vibrant display even during dry periods, conserves fresh water supplies, and saves on the water bill.

HOW TO DO IT

- Think desert: Many cacti, succulents, and yuccas naturally adapted to arid conditions will also grow—and even survive winter—in temperate zones, including prickly pears (*Opuntia*), hens and chicks or house leeks (*Sempervivum*), sedums, and Adam's needle (*Yucca filamentosa*). These plants are especially suited for easy-care container gardens on hot, sunny decks and patios.

- Look for plants with silver or gray leaves, many of which are drought tolerant, such as artemisias (*Artemisia* 'Powis Castle', *A. ludoviciana* 'Silver King', and *A. stelleriana*) yarrows (*Achillea*), and lamb's ears (*Stachys byzantina*).

- Given a year of TLC to establish themselves, perennials like baptisias, coneflowers (*Echinacea*), coreopsis, daylilies (*Hemerocallis*), black-eyed Susans (*Rudbeckia*), goldenrods (*Solidago*), and bee balm (*Monarda didyma*) will tolerate dry weather and bloom at different times through the summer and fall for nonstop color in the garden.

- For lots of color, plant annuals like rose moss (*Portulaca grandiflora*), nasturtium (*Tropaeolum majus*), salvias,

Recycled whiskey and wine barrels make attractive rustic rain collectors once they develop a weathered patina.

and cosmos, which happily bloom under dry conditions.

- While most established trees and shrubs can survive a season or two of unusually dry weather, many are naturally adapted to low-moisture conditions, including locust (*Gleditsia triacanthos*), junipers (*Juniperus*), white spruce (*Picea glauca*), dwarf mountain pine (*Pinus mugo*), hackberries (*Celtis*), kerrias, bush cinquefoil (*Potentilla fruticosa*), and rugosa rose (*Rosa rugosa*).

- Most sun-loving ornamental grasses are rugged enough to endure dry spells, including blue grama grass (*Bouteloua gracilis*), quaking grass (*Briza media*), and switch grass (*Panicum virgatum*).

15 Harvesting Rainwater

Untold gallons of rain beat down on roofs and are channeled into gutters and downspouts, straight into storm drains and streams. With just a little effort, much of that rain can be saved to irrigate your garden.

HOW TO DO IT

- An ideal water collector is a recycled whiskey or wine barrel. Look for them in nurseries, garden-supply stores, or nearby wineries. Don't worry if it leaks a bit at first; its seams will seal shut when it becomes waterlogged. Though not as attractive, a plastic trash can from your local hardware store will also work.

- The easiest and quickest way to use an unmodified barrel is to remove the top and place it beneath a downspout cut and angled to direct water into the barrel. You can always augment your system with downspout connectors, overflow valves, spigots, and other hardware.

- Make sure to devise some sort of a channel to direct overflow from the rain barrel away from the house. One option is to create a boggy swale garden where the overflow can drain. If you have a knack for simple plumbing, you can increase collection capacity by connecting several barrels with pipe or hoses. Standard garden-hose connectors simplify directing the overflow into drains or into the garden.

- Camouflage the barrel with a permanent planting of ornamental grasses, ferns, or tall-growing leafy tropicals

23

Using a simple tool like a rain gauge can help you maintain the "inch a week" moisture requirement in the garden.

Irrigating through slow seepage from punctured plastic jugs is efficient, sending water exactly where it's needed the most—the roots.

like elephant ears (*Caladium*), castor-oil plant (*Ricinus communis*), or cannas. Pots of bushy, tall annuals like zinnias, marigolds (*Tagetes*), or snapdragons (*Antirrhinum*) along with lower-growing plants like ageratum, coleus (*Solenostemon*), and sweet potato vine (*Ipomoea batatas*) can add extra color to the area.

16 Keeping Track of Rainfall

The rule of thumb for moisture in gardens in most temperate zones is an inch of rain a week. A rain gauge is a simple but effective tool for telling when you need to water, especially in the fall, when many plants are preparing to enter winter dormancy.

HOW TO DO IT

• Purchase or make a rain gauge and place it on the top edge of the garden fence or deck out of the way of trees, overhead wires, and roof edges. Check it once a week to measure exactly how much rain has fallen and irrigate your plants accordingly.

• Make a rain gauge by attaching with water-proof tape or glue a six-inch plastic ruler to the inside of a flat-bottomed, straight-sided glass or plastic jar. The mouth of the jar must be the same width as the jar itself.

17 Plastic Jug Irrigation

A gallon jug of water buried next to a fruit, vegetable, or newly planted shrub

Flexible and twiggy, spring-pruned fruit-tree branches are ideal for propping emerging peonies (left). To keep a tall-growing dahlia from flopping, set a tomato cage over it when it's six inches high.

is a great way to slowly deliver water where it's needed when rain is scarce.

HOW TO DO IT

- Make a small puncture in the bottom of a one-gallon plastic milk or juice jug, then bury it halfway up to its neck in the garden next to where you plan to plant water-loving fruits and vegetables like tomatoes, melons, squashes, and cucumbers.

- Plant seedlings next to the jug and water in the conventional way until the plant is established.

- Once the plant is growing, switch to plastic-jug watering by filling the jug with a hose or narrow-spouted watering can. The water will slowly trickle out of the hole down into the root zone. Before leaves hide the jug, mark its location with a tall stick.

- Irrigate established plants without disturbing the roots by placing the jug on top of the soil as close as possible to the plant.

- Occasionally substitute well-strained compost tea for water to give the plant a nutritional boost.

18 Supporting Tall Flowers

If there's anything sadder than the sight of an unsupported peony after a strong shower, it's a tall dahlia at the end of a windy day. Avoid these garden tragedies by putting in supports early in the season before the plants burgeon.

HOW TO DO IT

- Use slender, twiggy green-wood prunings from fruit trees and shrubs to prop up large bushy perennials like peonies (*Paeonia*) and lupines (*Lupinus*). In the spring when the stalk buds are just breaking through their mulch, encircle them with freshly cut branches approximately as tall as the plant will grow. Arrange the twigs so that they interlock for extra support. The growing foliage, and later the flowers, will hide them from sight. Once the supported plants are fully grown, clip off any twigs conspicuously taller than the plant.

• Less natural looking but quick and easy to set in place is a store-bought tomato cage. Place it into the soil around the emerging plant when the greenery is about six to ten inches high. It will look unsightly for a short time, but as the foliage grows upward it will hide the wires.

• Insert thin bamboo poles—available at garden-supply centers in lengths from one to six feet or more—alongside your dahlia tubers as you plant them. Tie the stems to the poles as they grow. Do the same for other tall flowers like lilies (*Lilium*), delphiniums, and foxgloves (*Digitalis*), tying the stakes to the bloom stalks before they begin to lean.

19 Protect Tree Trunks With Plants

Lawn mowers and string trimmers in the garden and dogs and cars along the street are just a few of the culprits that can cause nicks and gashes in tree bark and damage soil, weakening the tree and contributing to its demise. Surrounding a tree trunk with fast-

The bark and roots of this stewartia are protected from blades, boots, and pets by a ring of barrenwort.

This brick edging laid at ground level allows the mower to cut a tidy swath parallel to the bed.

growing groundcovers is an effective and attractive form of protection.

HOW TO DO IT

• Plant a circle of of shade-loving, fast-growing groundcovers like barren-worts (*Epimedium*), sweet woodruff (*Galium odoratum*), bugleweed (*Ajuga reptans*), or pachysandra around trees. They will recover from an overactive lawn mower or out-of-control string trimmer quicker than a shade tree will.

• For the protection of both the ground-cover and the tree, add a mulch edging between the lawn and plant circle, and leave a clear ring of soil near the base of the tree itself.

• Plant a ring of shade-tolerant annuals in a street-tree pit to signal passersby that somebody cares. This simple measure may get the tree more respect and inspire dog owners to give the tree a wide berth. Since flowers need regular watering, the tree will get a much-needed drink as well.

20 Edging Beds and Borders

Edging adds a neat, finishing touch to a garden bed or border and helps cut down on weeding due to lawn creep. If you're concerned about foot traffic, edging can also create a visual demarcation between the lawn, walk, or drive-way and your cultivated bed.

HOW TO DO IT

• A line of sharply cut sod at the edge of a lawn with a ribbon of earth between the grass and the bed is the

Prevent aggressive perennials like artemisias, tansy, and mints from spreading out of control by planting them in bottomless five-gallon pails.

easiest and one of the most attractive edgings. A variety of special sod-edging tools are available, but anything sharp that will cut cleanly through grass roots, like a garden spade or even a kitchen knife, will work.

• The quickest edging is steel, aluminum, plastic, or hard rubber strips pounded into the soil or set into a shallow trench between the grass and the garden bed.

• Another edging option is a mowing strip. It takes some time and effort to install, but once in place it will save time and work for years to come. Bricks laid side by side, concrete pavers laid end to end, or even a foot-wide strip of poured concrete

following the contour of the bed prevent the grass from spreading into the flower or vegetable bed. If set flush with or only slightly above the ground instead of at grass level, the edging provides a "roadway" for the lawn mower.

21 Containing Aggressive Plants

Some plants will take over if you let them. By containing their root system, most aggressively spreading plants, such as threadleaf coreopsis (*Coreopsis verticillata*), bishop's weed (*Aegopodium*), tansy (*Tanasetum vulgare*), artemisias, and members of the mint family, can be kept in their assigned garden seats.

Caladium bulbs started indoors can usually be planted outside when it's safe to set out tomatoes.

HOW TO DO IT

- To keep spreading plants confined, plant them in plastic pots buried up to their rims. Plant larger clumps in five-gallon plastic buckets buried to within two inches of their rims (first remove the bottom or drill holes in the bottom and sides of the pails for drainage). Or use chimney flues to contain exuberant plants (see Tip #58). For the most part, the plants will stay within the confines of their containers. However, some vigorous plants will take root if their stems grow or fall outside their confines and touch the soil. Rip out these upstarts without mercy.

- An even easier way to control some plants is not to introduce them to the garden in the first place. These plants, called invasive plants, are beyond aggressive. They can actually escape from your flower bed into the wild, damaging native habitats, other plants, and wildlife. Consider growing plants native to your area and conditions, since they are are less likely to grow out of bounds.

22 Giving Caladiums a Head Start

Showy tropical plants, caladiums thrive in the heat of summer. Enjoy their colorful glory earlier by starting them indoors four to eight weeks before outdoor planting time. This simple trick gives the bulbs time to develop a good root system, and their leaves will be well on their way to full size by the time you move them into the garden.

HOW TO DO IT

- Start the bulbs in a blend of soilless mix and compost, setting them in individual clay pots or mass planting them in plastic trays or recycled wooden fruit crates from the supermarket. Place the containers on a sunny windowsill or table in a room where the temperature stays around 70°F and keep the soil moist. The warmth and moisture bring the bulbs to life, and within a week tiny cones of growth begin to emerge.

- When leaf growth starts in earnest, move the plants to a sun-filled frost-free place or a sunny windowsill and be sure to keep the soil moist.

- After all danger of frost has passed, it's time to harden them off. Like tomatoes started indoors, caladiums need a week or two of weather adjustment in a sheltered spot to make the transition from the pampered warmth of the indoor environ-ment to the outdoor world's wind, rain, and variable temperatures.

23 Spring-Bulb Basics

A display of spring-flowering bulbs lightens the heart and can provide inspiration for the gardening season to come.

HOW TO DO IT

- Plant spring-flowering bulbs in the fall before the ground freezes. Prior to planting, amend the soil with compost and make sure that it drains well, especially if you'd like the bulbs to perennialize.

- Follow the "three times" rule: Plant each bulb three times as deep as the bulb is high (for example, plant a two-inch bulb six inches deep), and space the bulbs about three inches apart.

- For a grouping of daffodils (*Narcissus*) or tulips (*Tulipa*), dig a hole about a foot deep, fill the bottom four inches with compost, place the bulbs on top

---

Planting Spring Bulbs After It's Too Late

Fall, before the ground freezes, is bulb-planting time—ideally. But sometimes an end-of-season, 70-percent-off sale comes along and I can't resist, or else I simply procrastinate and find myself with a pile of unplanted daffodil, tulip, or hyacinth bulbs.

Anticipating this possibility, I deposit an eight-inch-deep layer of shredded leaves atop a compost-enriched garden bed where I might want some spring flowers. The leaves keep the soil beneath from freezing, and I can usually plant there long after the surrounding garden is rock solid. Several years ago on a frigid New Year's Day, I planted several dozen daffodils this way and was rewarded with a beautiful display toward the end of April. Bear in mind, however, that most hardy bulbs need about three months of cold and dark to trigger growth and flowering.

Instead of planting bulbs in rows, create a cluster effect by placing a dozen or so in one hole.

of this mixture, then cover with more compost. Plant the bulbs a couple of inches deeper in sandy soils. For smaller bulbs, such as glory-of-the-snow (*Chionodoxa luciliae*), crocuses, and Spanish bluebells (*Hyacinthoides hispanica*), dig the hole about eight inches deep.

- After planting, water the bulb bed, then cover it with mulch such as chopped leaves, straw, wood chips, or shredded bark. Usually fall rains will keep the bulbs watered, but if the rain doesn't come, water the bulbs once a week or so. Adequate moisture is essential for the bulbs to develop a good root structure in their early stage of growth.

- Fertilize well in early spring. After the bulbs have flowered, prune off the seed heads but don't remove the leaves—they supply nourishment for next year's bulbs.

- Plant spring-blooming bulbs among perennials, whose emerging foliage later in the season will gradually hide the yellowing bulb leaves.

- Plant annuals in between the waning bulbs to hide the foliage.

- Daffodils tend to multiply rapidly. If there are fewer flowers after a few years or if the blooms are smaller or nonexistent, the bed is probably crowded and needs to be replanted. Six to eight weeks after blooming, use

To keep daffodils blooming prolifically as they multiply, periodically dig up the clumps six weeks after flowering and replant the bulbs in soil freshly amended with compost.

a spading fork to dig up the entire bed and gently remove the bulbs. Apply several inches of compost and replant some of the bulbs, spacing them two to three inches apart. Cover with more compost and water. Plant the extra bulbs in another area or give them to a gardening friend.

• If you garden in an area where deer or squirrels are a problem, avoid growing tulips, which have especially tasty bulbs. Instead, plant snowdrops (*Galanthus*), daffodils, alliums, and grape hyacinths (*Muscari*), which deer eschew.

Improving the Soil

24 Winter Rye as a Cover Crop

Cover crops, also known as green manure, are an easy way to increase the fertility of garden soil. Planted in fall and turned under and blended with the soil in spring, they decompose and enhance the fertility and tilth of the earth. Use them in vegetable and annual gardens or any area that otherwise would be left bare over the winter.

HOW TO DO IT

• Winter rye (*Secale cereale*) is a popular cover crop for home gardeners (clover, alfalfa, vetch, and buckwheat are also used). In addition to improving the soil, its abundant top growth and root system keeps garden soil from eroding. Winter rye seed can be found at garden and farm-supply stores.

• Broadcast winter rye over the entire vegetable or annual garden in late summer to mid-fall, even among the still-growing plants. Scratch the large seeds into the soil where nothing is growing. Don't worry about the seeds scattered among the flowers and vegetables. They will germinate in the shade of the plants' leaves and firmly anchor themselves in the soil.

Winter rye sown among flowers and vegetables in the late-fall garden will enrich the soil when it's turned under the next spring.

Leaf mold forms naturally on the forest floor as successive seasons of decaying leaves compost to make a rich humus. You can speed up the process in your garden by shredding and moistening raked autumn leaves.

- Keep the rye seeds watered until they start showing growth. They germinate in four to six days, sending up slender red blades all over the garden. As the leaves grow they turn to bright green and will remain so all winter, even though the plants are dormant.

- In spring, growth resumes. Turn the rye under when it is about a foot high. After digging it in, wait two weeks to a month before planting. As it decomposes, the nitrogen-rich biomass improves the quality and fertility of the soil.

- You can also mow the rye or cut it down with a string trimmer and plant seedlings of early-spring greens and cabbages in among the green manure mulch. Using the cover crop as a mulch is good but not as beneficial as turning it under and incorporating it into the soil.

25 What to Do With Autumn Leaves

If you are fortunate enough to garden in the vicinity of deciduous trees, you can easily emulate nature and create your own supply of nutritious leaf mold—and put all those autumn leaves to good use.

HOW TO DO IT

- Collect leaves from lawns, walkways, sidewalks, and other areas where they aren't wanted. A leaf blower works quickly, but the leaves still have to be raked into piles for transport. A two-wheeled garden cart is far superior to a wheelbarrow for this purpose: It holds more, does not tip, is easier to push, and when tipped up to rest on the front end, it takes less storage space. A good tool for picking up piled leaves are two garbage-can lids. Holding one in each hand, spread your arms apart over the leaf pile, bury the lids in the pile vertically, then bring them together and lift the load of leaves into the cart.

- Another way to gather up the leaves is to rake them onto a plastic tarp or old bedsheet. After it's piled high, pick up the four corners to make a pouch and drag the leaves to their final destination (mower or leaf shredder and then compost pile or leaf mold pile).

- To make leaf mold, first gather fallen leaves and shred them. You can buy a machine that specializes in this, but a lawn mower set to high works just fine. If the mower lacks a collection-bag attachment, direct the mower to blow the leaf shreds against a wall or fence instead of across the yard. Rake the shredded leaves into a pile, turning and watering them occasionally to help them break down faster.

- Use leaf mold as a mulch around acid lovers like blueberries and azaleas.

- Blend leaf mold with sand, coconut fiber, and a little lime for potting mix.

- When transplanting, add a few generous handfuls of leaf mold to the bottom of the hole before inserting the plant in your garden soil.

26 Compost Fundamentals

Compost is a fantastic natural soil amendment that improves the quality of any garden soil and supports plant growth. But that's not the only advantage of this fabulous resource. It is super easy to make and it's free. For frugal gardeners—and what gardener isn't?—that should be reason enough to have a compost pile somewhere in the yard. (It is also worth noting that whatever stays in the garden doesn't need to find space in a burgeoning landfill.)

HOW TO DO IT

- Designate a spot for composting that's out of sight but not too long a hike

Making compost is as easy as mixing "green" and "brown" materials and keeping them moist and aerated while they cook.

from your kitchen. It should measure at least three feet by three feet.

- Ideally, keep two compost piles—one finished and ready for use and another for adding new material.

- Base your compost pile on a wooden pallet to improve ventilation and speed decomposition. They are often available free from nurseries and building-supply stores.

- Here's a trick for remembering compost basics: Think of the money you save when you use it. Specifically, think of a new $20 bill, which is mostly green, but to foil counterfeiters, is now tinged with a light brown. Green and brown are the colors of compost basics: The green stuff is usually "wet" and high in nitrogen. It includes grass clippings, kitchen waste, spent plants, even seaweed. The brown stuff is dry and rich in

carbon. It includes fallen leaves (preferably shredded), straw, hay, wood shavings, and corncobs. The key is to make sure there is both green and brown in your mix.

• Keep a small bucket or lidded pail in the kitchen for scraps destined for the compost pile, including vegetable and fruit waste, eggshells, used tea bags, and so on but not meat, fish, fats, pasta, or baked goods. (An exception to the vegetable-matter-only rule, human hair is high in nitrogen and okay to use.)

• Keep the pile moist at all times. It should not be soggy but nicely damp and spongy. Water as needed.

• Level the top of the pile, indenting it slightly toward the center to allow water to penetrate it efficiently.

• As you add new material to the compost pile, blend it with the old. Use a garden fork to aerate the pile every few weeks. Air is vital for the microbes that are breaking down the organic materials. (If the pile starts reeking, it has become anaerobic and needs to be turned immediately.) Since in warmer weather decomposi-

tion is faster than during the winter months, aerate more often in summer.

• To accelerate decomposition, add some finished compost to the fresh pile. The critters and the bacteria already living in the finished compost will help break down the raw materials.

• Use compost instead of commercial fertilizer: It releases its nutrients slowly over a long time period, and unlike commercial fertilizers, finished compost will never burn living plants.

• Compost helps dense clay soil drain more easily; conversely, it improves loose, sandy soils by slowing drainage.

• If you want a tidy compost area or need to keep animals out, you can build a compost bin: Construct an enclosure from snow fencing, wooden skids, wire fencing, cement blocks (see Tip #93), straw bales, wooden boards, or simply use an ordinary garbage can with holes punched in the walls and lid for ventilation.

• There are also plenty of ready-made composters on the market. Especially useful in small gardens are compact models with a footprint of one square yard. Load the raw materials at the

The Easiest Way to Compost

Instead of using a composter or starting a pile, you can spread the organic materials in different places of your yard as a mulch, or spread the material to be composted and cover it with a layer of soil. Called sheet composting, this works especially well if you spread the materials in the fall, giving them time to convert to humus through the winter. It's a good way to get rid of all those fallen leaves. (If you've been using an organic mulch on any part of your garden, you've been sheet composting.)

Extend your valuable supply of compost with chopped leaves or grass clippings when planting something large like a tree or shrub.

top and retrieve finished compost through an opening in the front. One word of advice: Stay away from fancy drums and tumblers. They are expensive and don't produce any better compost than other methods.

27 Making Compost Last Longer

Most gardeners never have enough compost. Here are some ways to make the most of this king of soil conditioners.

HOW TO DO IT

• To maximize a limited supply of compost, use it sparingly, by the trowelful. When transplanting seedlings into the garden, carry a bucket of compost along. For each plant, scoop out enough soil to accommodate the roots of the plant, plus a trowelful more. Replace that trowelful of soil with an equivalent amount of compost. Insert the seedling, add more compost, gently tamp down the soil around the plant, and water. The plant will grow rapidly in the loose, nutritious compost.

• Herbs, perennials, trees, and shrubs need bigger planting holes and more compost. To stretch your supply, add shredded leaves or dried grass clippings to it. After planting larger specimens, mulch the plants with straw, chopped leaves, leaf mold, or shredded bark. Eventually, as these organics break down, they will further enrich the soil.

28 A Recipe for Compost Tea

In addition to using dry compost to enhance your soil, you can make it into a liquid fertilizer called compost tea.

HOW TO DO IT

Fill one third of a five-gallon plastic bucket with compost, then add water to the brim and stir. Let the bucket sit and steep for two days, stirring occasionally. To use, strain and then dilute the tea concentrate with enough water to turn it about the same color as apple juice. Use the compost tea to water newly planted seeds and transplants, houseplants, and container plants growing outdoors.

29 Lasagna Gardening

The practice of lasagna gardening, codified by Patricia Lanza in three books,

After this new bed has "cooked" for a couple of months, the plastic can be removed for planting.

revives an old method of creating planting beds aboveground from layers of organic material.

HOW TO DO IT

- Select an area to be planted and mow it if necessary. Cover it with a layer of eight to ten sheets of newspaper, then thoroughly soak it with water.

- Cover the newspapers with several one- to five-inch layers of organic material, such as grass clippings, pulled weeds, leaf mold, chopped leaves, seaweed, horse manure or used stable bedding (straw or sawdust), compost, and anything else that will easily decompose. Build the bed up to

A Late-Season Lasagna Garden

I once started a fall vegetable garden from scratch in the middle of August using the lasagna gardening method. In my Zone 6 New Jersey garden, this was pushing the envelope: I had only 60 days before the first anticipated frost. After dumping about a dozen loads of finished compost directly on the sod, I raked it smooth and made raised beds of varying sizes. Some were seeded; others were planted with seedlings transplanted from other parts of the garden. The balance of August was warm, as was September, and the frost we usually get in mid-October held off until the end of the month. That fall garden gave us cool-weather vegetables—turnips, radishes, kohlrabi, spinach, and assorted salad greens—for our Thanksgiving dinner, and by sheltering some of the beds from the cold, we enjoyed fresh-from-the-garden salads until late December.

at least 12 inches. Next, wet the planting bed down and cover it with plastic, preferably black. Let the covered bed "cook" for about two months. The result will be a rich, dark, crumbly soil, ready for planting.

- If you create a raised planting bed with a deep layer made entirely from finished compost (see Tip #4), you can bypass the two-month waiting period and start your garden right away.

30 What, When, and How to Mulch

A deciduous forest is a good place to see how mulch works. Year after year, the trees shed their leaves, which fall and cover the forest floor. This layer of slowly decomposing leaves protects the ground around the trees from erosion; holds moisture, protects the forest floor from extreme heat and cold, and keeps weeds from germinating. What nature does in the forest you can do in your garden.

HOW TO DO IT

- Organic mulches are the most useful to gardeners. They eventually decompose and add humus to the soil. Two of the most readily available to most of us are grass clippings and leaves. Depending on where you live, regionally popular organic mulches include straw, seaweed, peanut hulls, shredded bark, chopped-up corncobs, and pine needles.

- Spread a two- to three-inch layer of mulch over all cultivated areas in your garden to slow erosion and discourage weeds. Mulch also helps regulate the temperature of the soil, keeping it cool in the heat of summer and holding its warmth in fall. It also conserves soil moisture, an important consideration during droughts or in areas where rainfall is scarce.

- Put an additional thick layer of organic mulch on your vegetable beds in fall to extend vegetable harvests beyond the normal growing season.

- In regions with cold winters, add an extra layer of organic mulch to the perennial beds once the ground is frozen solid. As soil alternately freezes and thaws, plants can be heaved out of the soil, which exposes their roots to chilling, drying winds and eventually kills them. When mulched, the soil stays frozen and the roots remain firmly anchored. Timing is important: If you apply the mulch before the ground is frozen, rodents and other critters will be drawn to its warmth and they'll eat what the mulch is supposed to protect.

- Saw off the branches of your Christmas tree to use as mulch on perennials. If your saw gums up with sap, wipe down the blade with a pine-oil-based household cleaner.

- Use mulch to smother weeds: Cover a new or overgrown bed with a layer of newspaper, wet it down, and camouflage it with a more attractive mulch like grass clippings, chopped leaves, or wood chips. Within six to eight weeks you should have a clean growing area. This method also works for keeping weeds down between garden rows.

- In addition to organic mulches, just about anything that covers the soil to block weeds can be used as a mulch, including pebbles, roofing shingles, carpeting, black plastic, and boards.

31 Making Use of Wood Ash

Save the ashes from your fireplace or woodstove for your garden. Depending on the type of wood burned, ashes can be a good source of calcium, potassium, and phosphorus and act as a liming agent for acidic soil.

HOW TO DO IT

- Through the wood-burning months, collect and store the ashes for use during planting time in an ashcan or metal bucket with a watertight cover. Be sure to transfer the ashes to the storage can only after they have completely cooled.

- Don't be tempted to scatter the ashes on the garden before the growing season. Snow and rains will leach away the nutrients, providing little or no value to the soil. Instead, work the ashes into the soil before spring planting (experts recommend using 10 to 20 pounds of ash per 1,000 square feet of soil).

- Wood ash acts like lime as a soil deacidifier and is stronger in the short run, so be sparing and careful in application to avoid making the soil too alkaline. It's always a good idea to do a soil pH test every other year before applying wood ash.

- Scatter wood ash around the base of vegetables such as cabbages and onions to discourage root maggots. Surface pests like slugs and snails are also repelled by a layer of ashes.

- Use wood ash as a side dressing for alkaline-loving plants such as clematis, hellebores, and succulents. Scatter a small amount in a circle around (never on) growing plants.

- Wood ashes reduce soil acidity and should not be used around acid-loving plants like rhododendrons, blueberries (*Vaccinium*), or potatoes (*Solanum tuberosum*).

Collect wood ash for use as a pest control and as side dressing around alkaline-loving plants.

Pest Controls

32 Attracting Birds, the Ultimate Insecticide

The more birds that hang out in your garden the fewer bugs you'll have. Birds have a voracious appetite, and the many insects that feast on the plants in your garden are some of their favorite spring and summer foods.

HOW TO DO IT

• To attract birds, provide water, especially on scorching-hot summer days, during dry spells, and throughout the winter months. Fill a birdbath or another shallow container with an inch or two of fresh water every day to keep them coming. Clean the container once a week.

• To make the birdbath even more user-friendly, put a flat rock in the center of the pool. Along with the rim, this gives the birds a place to rest, drink, and bathe.

• Set out one or more bird feeders. Check with your local Audubon Center if you are not sure which birds are prevalent in your area and what kind of seeds might attract them.

• Sprinkle a little birdseed (except sunflower seeds) around plants that are preyed on by chewing insects. The birds will eat the seeds for their entree and have the bugs for dessert. They will dispose of Japanese beetles on

---

Conifers for the Birds

My first vegetable garden was planted alongside an open hayfield. It was bug paradise until I planted a stand of conifers as a windbreak on the upsloping western side to create a more favorable microclimate. And there was an extra bonus: As the evergreens slowly increased in size, I noticed that the bird population also increased and the bug population went down. The trees gave insect-eating birds resting places, nesting sites, and shelter from predators (above all, cats).

A pool of fresh water is an irresistible lure for birds, who will quench their thirst, take a bath, and proceed to rid your yard of pesky bugs.

which may only be practical for small potted plants indoors, and using toxic chemicals. Made from potassium salts of fatty acids, insecticidal soap is most often applied as a water-diluted spray. The soap damages soft-bodied insects' cell membranes, dehydrating and killing pests covered by it. Once the spray dries, it's no longer effective.

HOW TO DO IT

- To maximize the effectiveness of insecticidal soap outdoors, spray early in the morning when the plants are still dew covered or late in the afternoon or after sunset. Avoid spraying at midday in the hot sun—the soap will dry before it can work.

- Whether you are using the spray outdoors or indoors, be sure to douse both sides of the leaves; many pests feed from the undersides of leaves or take shelter there if they detect movement or light changes indicating danger.

- Since insecticidal soap only works while it's wet, spray several times a week for three weeks. A visual inspection will tell you when it's time to resume spraying.

- Make your own insecticidal soap by adding two tablespoons of a vegetable-oil-based liquid soap such as castile soap to a gallon of water. Don't use laundry detergent or liquid dish soap, which may contain dyes and chemicals that are harmful to your plants. But even if you choose to buy

roses and grapes, Mexican bean beetles on beans, tiny black flea beetles on eggplants.

- To keep birds near your garden year-round, plant trees and shrubs that provide shelter and food. Berry-producing native shrubs such as dogwoods (*Cornus*), viburnums, serviceberry or shadbush (*Amelanchier*), and American bittersweet (*Celastrus scandens*) are good, bird-friendly choices.

- If trees or shrubs are not an option, set out stakes around your yard to give birds places to rest and flee if startled.

33 Safe, Easy Insecticidal Soaps

Insecticidal soaps are a happy compromise between spraying plants with water to dislodge harmful pests (see Tip #69),

A bottomless paper cup inserted in the ground with the rim just above soil level helps prevent cutworms from chewing through the stems of delicate seedlings such as this cabbage.

insecticidal soap, the investment isn't going to break the bank. Sold as a concentrate, it generally calls for two teaspoons of soap per pint of water. You'll get a lot of sprays for your investment—and fewer bugs!

34 Saving Seedlings With Cutworm Collars

Easy-to-make "collars" will prevent newly planted members of the cabbage family such as broccoli, kale, and collards, as well as seedlings of tomatoes, beans, corn, peppers, and strawberries, from being destroyed by cutworms. As their name implies, these pests chew into the delicate stems of the young plants at the soil line, nibble a bit, then go on to the next plant. In a single night they can wipe out an entire row of seedlings.

HOW TO DO IT

• Plant each seedling inside a half-buried bottomless paper cup. Or make collars out of tar paper, corrugated cardboard, or another material.

• Alternatively, push a four-inch nail into the soil right up against the stem of the seedling. It discourages the cutworms from munching.

35 Cabbageworm Protection

Floating row covers suspended over young plants protect broccoli, brussels sprouts, cauliflower, and other members of the cabbage family against cabbageworms. These are the caterpillars of a small white butterfly, appropriately called the cabbage white (*Pieris rapae*). When you see the butterflies fluttering

Floating row covers installed right after planting protect cabbages, cauliflower, and other brassicas against damage from cabbageworms.

cas in your garden for telltale holes in the leaves, the damage wreaked by the small green cabbage white caterpillars. Cabbageworms are about an inch long and have the girth of a wooden matchstick. They are well camouflaged, so most likely you will see their damage before you see the caterpillars themselves. Once you spot one, pick it off by hand and destroy it.

• If you're squeamish about picking off cabbageworms, dislodge them with a gentle stream from the garden hose, then dispatch them.

• In addition to the preemptive advantage that using row covers has over handpicking caterpillars, you won't inadvertently kill other species of future butterflies that might be beneficial in your garden.

among your brassicas, they're laying eggs, which will hatch within about a week. The emergent caterpillars will immediately start chomping, making short work of any cabbage-family members in their path unless you get active.

HOW TO DO IT

• If the butterflies can't land on the plants, they won't be able to lay their eggs on them. Cover young transplants and seedlings of members of the cabbage family with lightweight row covers like Reemay or Agronet right after planting. To keep the featherlight covers from blowing away, anchor them with stones or bend wire clothes hangers into U-shaped pins and use these to anchor the covers to the ground.

• If you don't get around to covering the plants right away, check all brassi-

36 Keeping Slugs Under Control

Slugs are voracious eaters that quickly devour seedlings or any other fresh succulent plant growth in their paths. Two options: Attract, collect, and dispose of them or deter them by creating a slug-unfriendly environment.

HOW TO DO IT

• Bury a shallow tin such as a tuna or cat-food can up to the rim in the soil. Fill it with beer and check regularly to remove slugs that have been attracted to the beer and drowned.

- Sprinkle diatomaceous earth, wood ashes, or fine sand around vulnerable plants. The dry, sharp-edged material deters the soft-bodied critters.

- The easiest method: Lay a wide board alongside plants that need protection. Slugs will be attracted by the darkness and dampness that the underside of the board offers. Every morning turn the board over and zap all the slugs lurking there.

37 Deer Deterrents That Work

Once roaming open fields and forests and controlled by natural predators, deer now must make their home near housing developments, office parks, and shopping malls, and their populations are growing. Little wonder then that they treat our gardens like buffet bars. Thoughtful plant choices, fences, dogs, and repellents help to keep deer at bay.

HOW TO DO IT

- As a first line of defense, line paths and garden borders with deer-repelling plants such as alliums and aromatic herbs like mints (*Mentha*), lavenders (*Lavandula*), sages (*Salvia*), and thyme (*Thymus*). If that first nibble smells or tastes nasty, the deer may just move on without venturing further into the garden.

- Woody plants like boxwood (*Buxus*), spireas (*Spiraea*), rhododendrons, and blue spruce (*Picea pungens*); annuals such as ageratum, celosias, cleomes, marigolds (*Tagetes*), and zinnias; and herbaceous perennials like coreopsis, lupines (*Lupinus*), and poppies (*Papaver*), touted by nurseries as "deer resistant," are just that. Do deer stay away from these plants? That depends on how hungry they are. They do seem to avoid many ornamental grasses and silver-leafed or fuzzy plants like artemisias, dusty miller (*Senecio cineraria*), and lamb's ears (*Stachys byzantia*).

- Avoid planting tulips, a deer favorite, use daffodils (*Narcissus*) instead. They are noxious to deer.

- Fence deer out: An eight-foot-high wire or plastic fence is effective but unsightly and expensive. Less aesthetically challenging, an electric fence

Dog Versus Deer

Years ago I had a Bouvier and later a mutt, which were free to roam my farm during the day but were kept indoors at night. Whenever the dogs spotted deer, they gave chase. They never caught up with any, but their presence was enough to deter the deer from foraging in my yard at night, when they usually do most of their damage.

Invisible electronic dog fencing installed along the periphery of the property is a good way to keep a pet from straying. The dog wears an electronic collar that gives it a mild shock when it crosses a buried wire. After as short training session, the dog learns not to cross the buried electric fence.

Arched over tasty vegetable crops, wire fencing discourages hungry deer.

tal plants that deer favor (not recommended for vegetable or herb gardens).

• Check with other gardeners in your area about their success with commercial products and regimes of alternating deer repellents before you purchase one or more products such as Living Fence, Hinder, Deer Off, Deer Away, Bobbex, or coyote urine.

38 Using Kitchen Supplies to Control Weeds

Some of the weeds in your yard and garden can be spot controlled with materials grabbed on a quick trip to the kitchen.

HOW TO DO IT

• Scald individual weeds, such as ones growing in sidewalk and patio cracks, by pouring boiling water in a stream directly over the plant; perennial weeds may take two or three applications over time. For small patches, apply boiling water, then quickly cover the "hot spot" with a thick layer of mulch or other insulating material (newspapers or black plastic) for a few days to finish the job.

• Vinegar applied with a spray bottle can kill many common leafy weeds. The higher the acid concentration, the more effective it is. Most culinary vinegars have about 5 percent acidity and may require multiple applications; try pickling vinegar, which usually has about 10 percent acidity.

with just a single strand of wire works perhaps 90 percent of the time. In the vegetable garden, arch two-by-four-inch-mesh wire fencing over vulnerable produce. The arches can be moved for working on the beds or harvesting.

• Even better than a fence is a dog, provided the dog is at liberty and willing to give chase to the deer.

• If you use scent and taste repellents, alternate them frequently.

• Stuff the toe of a cut-off panty hose leg with a handful of human hair and suspend it near a vulnerable plant.

• Hang bars of scented soap in trees and shrubs prone to deer browse.

• Apply a spray made by mixing water with crushed garlic, old eggs, and hot pepper sauce around vulnerable plants.

• Scatter Milorganite, a fertilizer made from sewer effluent, around ornamen-

Propagation

39 Making More African Violets

Why be satisfied with just a pot or two of African violets (*Saintpaulia ionantha*) when you can have dozens? Try multiplying your plants from leaf cuttings, and use the "pot-in-a-pot" method to take the guesswork out of watering by providing the delicate cuttings with just the right amount of water they need.

HOW TO DO IT

• Fill a shallow, eight-inch-wide clay flower pot with a moist sterile soilless mix like Pro-mix or Jiffy-mix. To facilitate drainage, add a few generous pinches of horticultural sand or grit to the mix. Do not use garden soil— it packs too tightly if used in a pot.

• Plug the drainage hole of a three-inch-wide clay pot with a cork and bury the pot up to its rim in the center of the mix in the larger pot.

• Harvest leaves from a vigorously growing "mother" African violet plant with about an inch of leaf stem attached. If you plan to start numerous new plants, gather leaves from several mother plants to avoid completely denuding a single plant.

• Using a pencil, make a hole in the soil of the larger pot, dip a leaf stem in rooting hormone, insert it into the hole, and gently compact the soil around the stem to eliminate air pockets. Continue with the other leaves, space them an inch or so apart in the area between the rim of the big pot and the smaller pot.

• Fill the small pot in the center with water. The porosity of the clay pot will allow the water to slowly seep into the soil, keeping it evenly moist, which encourages rooting. Do not add water directly to the soil. As needed, replenish the water in the small center pot to keep it full to the brim. Avoid getting water on the leaves, which can encourage fungal infections.

To root African violets, place a small pot in a larger container and surround it with leaf cuttings. When the smaller pot is filled with water, it will keep the developing plants evenly moist.

• Move the pot to a spot that's about 70°F and generally favorable for growing African violets: It should receive bright light but no direct sunlight. An east or north window works well, but avoid drafts and keep the plants at a safe distance from cold window panes.

• In a few weeks you'll see tiny leaves surrounding each of the big parent leaves. Give the new African violet plants another 10 to 20 days to grow a larger root system. Test for root development by gently giving one of the tiny plants a tug. If there is some resistance, the leaf stem has devel-oped roots and the new plant is ready for transplanting into a four-inch pot.

40 Dividing Clumps of Herbaceous Perennials

Increase your collection of herbaceous perennials by dividing mature clumps. Most herbaceous perennials can be divided every few years, and many actually benefit from it. The time for dividing has come when flowers start getting smaller; when the plants spread beyond their allocated space or get crowded; or when the center of a clump starts dying out.

HOW TO DO IT

- Divide spring- and summer-blooming perennials in fall and fall bloomers in spring.

- In autumn, try to get divisions planted at least six weeks before the ground freezes. Once the ground is frozen, mulch them with straw or chopped leaves to keep the plants from being heaved out of the soil by alternating cycles of freezing and thawing.

- In spring, divide perennials as soon as you see new growth peeking out of the soil. Your objective is to allow the new divisions enough time to get established before the heat of summer. If divisions are at least fist size, most of the new transplants will bloom that year, but they may be a little behind schedule.

- Whether you divide in spring or fall, always do some prepping ahead of time. Determine where the divided plant is to go, dig a hole, and cover the bottom with a three-inch layer of compost. Thoroughly water the plant to be divided two days ahead of time. Watch the weather and pick a cloudy, even drizzly day to do the job.

- Depending on the plant and its size, either dig up the entire clump and split it into smaller sections with a sharp spade or slice a chunk off a crowded clump. Shake off some of the soil clinging to the division,

Large clumps of many herbaceous perennials, such as these irises, can easily be divided every few years to make more plants.

untangle the roots, and plant it immediately in the new hole at the same depth at which it was growing before. Cover with compost, gently tamp down the soil to get rid of air pockets, and water. Prune stems and foliage back slightly. If a section of a divided perennial is to go back in its original location, enrich the soil with compost.

- If a maximum number of new plants is your objective when dividing, hose all the soil off the clump and expose the roots. Try teasing the tangled roots apart into individual crowns, or cut them apart with a knife, leaving a crown on each section. These small divisions may will take at least a year to establish and probably won't bloom until the year after that.

- Use a sharp knife to divide the tuberous roots of dahlias and peonies. Cut

To root cuttings from tender perennials such as geraniums, fill a pot with soilless potting mix, dip the cutting in rooting hormone, make a hole in the mix, and insert the cutting.

in such a way that at least one growth bud is attached to each section.

• Some perennials, such as asters, 'Silver King' wormwood (*Artemisia* 'Silver King'), chrysanthemums, and coreopsis, spread rapidly and should be divided every year or two to keep them in bounds.

• Bleeding hearts (*Dicentra*), hostas, red hot poker (*Kniphofia*), lily-of-the-valley (*Convallaria*), and peonies don't need to be divided unless you would like additional plants or they're taking up too much space in your garden.

41 Overwintering Plants With Cuttings

Say you want to overwinter a tender perennial from your garden but don't have room inside for the entire plant. By taking a cutting and rooting it, you can preserve your plant in miniature form and have it ready to go back into the ground or garden container by spring.

HOW TO DO IT

• Gather together small pots, rooting hormone (liquid or powder), and soilless potting mix. Fill each pot with well-moistened potting mix to within half an inch of the lip. Using a dibble, pencil, or fingertip, poke a hole into the mix two to three inches deep.

• For each plant you wish to root, take a six-inch cutting from the tip of the plant, making the cut just above a node (where leaves branch out from the stem). Remove the growing tip

A partly buried branch of this Russian sage (*Perovskia atriplicifolia*) will soon form its own roots.

and the bottom set of leaves from the cutting. Dip the stem end into rooting hormone up to where you pinched off the bottom leaves and tap off any excess. Insert the stem into the prepared hole in your pot and firm the mix around it.

• Water the cutting and then provide additional humidity by misting or enclosing the pot with clear plastic wrap. New top growth will indicate that roots have formed and the plant can be transplanted. To keep your new plants in bounds through the winter, pinch back the growing tips.

• Cuttings work for tender perennials grown as annuals such as coleus, fuchsias, pelargoniums, passionflowers (*Passiflora*), and hyssops (*Agastache*).

42 Making More Woody Perennials

Some woody ornamental plants and herbs in your garden can be propagated by the easy process of layering, in which you grow a new plant from a branch that remains attached to the original plant. Good candidates for layering include hydrangeas, azaleas (*Rhododendron*), rhododendrons, weigelas, and rosemary (*Rosmarinus officinalis*).

HOW TO DO IT

• Choose a branch close to the ground. At the middle of the branch, use your fingernail or a knife to remove about an inch of bark from its underside.

• With the branch still attached to the plant, place the bared branch section

To test old seeds' viability, roll a few in a moist paper towel, seal in a bag, and store in a warm place. After about ten days, count those that have sprouted to determine the germination rate.

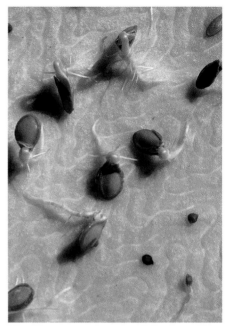

under the soil surface and curve the branch tip up out of the ground to form a U-shape. Place a stone on top of the debarked section of the branch to keep it buried underground, or anchor it in place with a giant "hairpin" made from a wire coat hanger.

• Give the plant about a year to develop a good root system, which will develop from the buried section.

• When you are ready to separate the new plant, water the soil around it well, wait a day, then nip it off the mother plant. Dig it up with a good ball of soil and plant it in a prepared hole.

• Layer propagate at any time in the growing season. If you're in a hurry, layer the branch early in spring. It should be rooted and ready to move by the end of summer.

43 Keeping Seeds Viable

With proper storage, most seeds stay viable for several years—you needn't throw them away just because the expiration date on the seed packet has come and gone. Before planting older seeds, do a simple test to determine how well they germinate.

HOW TO DO IT

• To keep seeds viable as long as possible, store them in dry, airtight jars or plastic zipper bags in the refrigerator or freezer. Be sure to label the bags with the names of the plants and the dates.

• To test old seeds, count out ten on a double thickness of moistened paper towel. Roll up the towel, place it in a plastic bag, seal it with a twist tie, and move it to a warm place (about 70°F to 80°F). In six to ten days, open the package to check for germination. If half the seeds have germinated, the germination rate is 50 percent. To make up for the reduced rate of germination, simply sow twice as many seeds as you otherwise would.

44 An East Way to Start Seeds

It's easy to start annuals or vegetables from seed. All you need are a few supplies and a sunny windowsill. Shopping for seeds offers you many more choices than buying nursery-propagated stock

Egg cartons make handy seed-starting trays: At transplanting time, break up and discard polystyrene cartons. Cut apart and crush pressed-paper cartons and put them in the soil with the seedlings.

and costs a lot less. By using homemade seed-starting trays and plastic-bag green-houses, you can save even more.

HOW TO DO IT

• Redeploy pressed-paper egg cartons as seed-starting trays. Their little cups are just the right size to hold tiny seedlings. Pressed paper holds up long enough for the seeds to germinate and start grow-ing but breaks down easily in the soil, which means it's not necessary to dis-turb the delicate root systems when transplanting seedlings into the garden.

• Use a nail to punch a hole in the bot-tom of each egg compartment. Cut off the carton lid and use it as a tray underneath the seedlings.

• Fill the compartments with moistened sterile seed-starting mix. Place three seeds in each and barely cover them with mix. Place the carton in a plastic bag and store it in a warm place.

• When the seeds germinate, remove the plastic bag and move the carton to a bright windowsill, but avoid too much direct sunlight—glass panes magnify the sun's intensity.

• After about two weeks, use scissors to snip off (but don't pull out) all but the strongest seedling from each sec-tion. Keep the seedlings moist and apply liquid organic fertilizer at a quarter strength when you water. When two sets of true leaves have emerged, move up to one-third strength.

• About four to six weeks after germi-nation, harden off the seedlings in a sheltered spot outdoors for a week before they are planted in the garden. Then cut the carton apart, gently crush each section, and put the seedling in the ground, carton and all, to avoid disturbing the roots.

• Save money: A packet of seeds and a six-pack of seedlings cost roughly the same. The six-pack gives you exactly six plants, a packet of seeds will give you double, triple, even ten times as many plants to use in your own garden or share with other gardeners.

• Start seeds of cold-weather crops such as lettuces, beets, and radishes indoors in late winter to have seedlings ready to set out as soon as the weather permits. This will give you a four- to six-week head start over the seeds that you plant directly in the vegetable garden at the same time, allowing an extended harvest.

45 Thinning for Healthy Seedlings

Unless you plant seeds in individual containers, thinning seedlings is absolutely essential to avoid stunted plant growth.

HOW TO DO IT

• Thin a row or flat of crowded seedlings by snipping out the weakest ones with scissors to avoid disturbing the roots of the remaining plants.

• If you're intent upon keeping all the seedlings that sprout, reduce crowding by repotting them individually 20 to 25 days after germination. Seedlings survive this method better than they do when left to grow thickly for weeks before being transplanted. Use this method for crowded garden-grown seedlings too. Fill egg cartons or six-packs with moist, sterile soil mix and make a finger hole in each section. Gently separate the roots of the seedlings with a pencil, lift each plant by a fragile leaf (not its stem), insert it into a hole, and carefully pack with soil. Grow the plants in the packs for a few weeks until you've found a new home for them.

• Avoid thinning by seeding thinly. To evenly distribute tiny seeds like carrots, lettuces, beets, celosias, or poppies, half fill a saltshaker with superfine sand and mix in your seeds. Sprinkle the sand along a prepared garden row or broadcast in a patch.

Thinning seedlings encourages strong plant growth, and, in the case of carrots, provides plenty of room for succulent roots to grow.

Garden Design

46 Creating a Garden Plan the Easy Way

Repositionable stickers like Post-It notes are handy for any gardener planning a new bed or border. Moving around flower photos attached to sticky notes on a garden plan is a lot easier than digging up and moving the plants themselves later on.

HOW TO DO IT

- Before putting a spade in the ground, sketch a rough layout of your new garden, then peruse current garden catalogs to make your initial plant selection.

- Cut out pictures from old garden catalogs of the plants you want in your garden, tape them to sticky notes, and arrange them on your plan. If colors clash or if there is too much sameness in height or texture, simply lift the plant sticker and switch its location, substitute it for another plant, or eliminate it entirely.

- Use pictures of plants in various seasons to see how your new garden bed will look throughout the year.

47 Providing Fall Color With Hardy Annuals

By Labor Day, a lot of summer-blooming annuals have begun to show their age: Time to compost them and replace them with annuals that thrive as the weather turns cooler.

HOW TO DO IT

- One of the most durable and colorful annuals isn't a flower but a cabbage. Sometimes called flowering kales, these brassicas are impressive, especially when planted in masses. Ranging from variegated white and green to pink to deep purple, some of these ornamental cabbages resemble giant roses and others look like ferns. To have the cabbages in full "bloom" in fall, start them around mid-June using the same method you would for conventional edible cabbage (see Tip

For a splash of color in the fall garden, replace spent summer annuals with ornamental cabbages. They welcome the cooler temperatures, looking spiffy through the first frost and beyond.

#44). But if you don't get around to starting them early, look for potted plants at garden centers beginning in September.

• Colorful, low-growing pansies (*Viola* × *wittrockiana*) are perfect to use as edging in a fall border planting. Best of all, they usually rebloom in early spring—in Zone 7 and warmer they might even bloom throughout the winter.

• Snapdragon (*Antirrhinum majus*), a short-lived perennial, is considered a hardy annual by gardeners because it can tolerate light frost and even a little snow. Plant dwarf varieties just behind the edging pansies in fall, with taller cultivars placed behind these.

Snapdragons also make great cutting flowers for indoor bouquets.

• Dusty miller (*Senecio cineraria*) is another hardy choice for the fall border; it can often overwinter in cool but mostly frost-free climates. It also makes a nice foliage filler for fall flower arrangements: The aptly named cultivar 'Silver Lace' has delicate lacy leaves that are especially useful.

• Tall cosmos is a very durable annual for the back of the border and looks good until zapped by frost. The flowers range in color from cool whites and pinks to the hot yellows and oranges of *Cosmos sulphureus* cultivars. A big plus of cosmos is that it is a prolific bloomer and doesn't require constant deadheading.

48 Keeping Borders Colorful

Does your garden suffer from those dreary in-between periods when some perennials have finished blooming and others have yet to flower? Colorful annuals are great for temporarily livening up spots in beds and borders that may periodically become devoid of interest.

HOW TO DO IT

• You can always run to the local garden center to buy annuals. But you can save money and improve your choices by planning ahead. Early in the season, start some extra seeds or buy flats of small plants—marigolds (*Tagetes*), salvias, zinnias, and begonias are good choices. Keep them in pots or in a few rows in an out-of-the-way area or in your vegetable garden. Over the summer, move the pots or transplant the plants to beds and borders that need a splash of color.

• Don't limit your plant choices to ornamental flowers. Chile peppers (*Capsicum annuum* cultivars), purple-leafed okra (*Abelmoschus esculentus* 'Burgundy'), Swiss chard (*Beta vulgaris*), and red-stemmed Malabar spinach (*Basella alba* 'Rubra'), among others, are quite decorative and have the added advantage of being edible!

• You can also move potted houseplants outdoors when some splashes of color or interesting foliage are needed. Place the pots in a sheltered spot for a few days to let the plants adapt to the wind and stronger light of the great outdoors. After that they should benefit from the fresh air and natural light.

49 Creating Vertical Accents

To spark up your flower garden, put in some exclamation points—plants that tower above adjacent plants and help create a wave effect, leading the eye first up and then down. The more vertical variety there is in a garden, the more interesting it is. Think of the New York City skyline and imagine how drab it would be if the buildings were uniformly level. Differences in plant height will keep your garden's "skyline" more interesting.

HOW TO DO IT

• Available in many different sizes, ornamental grasses make excellent exclamation points. Most grow to around five or six feet tall, which is perfect for the average garden. Two excellent upright growers are 'Heavy Metal' switch grass (*Panicum virgatum* 'Heavy Metal') and 'Karl Foerster' feather reed grass (*Calamagrostis* × *acutiflora* 'Karl Foerster').

• Plants with showy flowers that make attractive vertical statements include foxtail lilies (*Eremurus*), sunflowers (*Helianthus*), fragrant flowering tobacco (*Nicotiana sylvestris*), joe-pye weeds (*Eupatorium*), and goldenrods (*Solidago*).

Peeking out from a mass of foliage and waving gently in the breeze, the brightly colored flower spikes of foxtail lilies give this planting a playful touch while adding vertical interest.

• Some lilies (*Lilium*) grow to four feet but might need some support (see Tip #18), as will dahlias and delphiniums.

• Cannas have variously green, yellow, maroon, and almost black leaves that reach to three to four feet, and later in the season the flower stalk adds another foot or two to their height. Plant cannas in the ground at the rear of a border or in pots as moveable accents.

• Crown imperial (*Fritillaria imperialis*), a spring-flowering bulb, grows to about three feet when in bloom. This may not sound that tall, but when they flower, they tower over other early bloomers, adding vertical variety to the garden. And their skunky aroma may keep deer away from nearby tulips.

50 Low-Maintenance Plantings for Slopes

Replacing turfgrass with a groundcover on a slope reduces maintenance (no mowing!), saves time, and may even prevent injury. (Accidents can occur when gardeners underestimate the slickness of grass and slip when mowing a slope.) And a well-chosen groundcover usually looks a lot more interesting than plain grass.

HOW TO DO IT

• Plant slopes with perennial groundcovers that fill in quickly. Imagine an entire bank of creeping phlox (*Phlox stolonifera*) in glorious spring bloom. Daylilies (*Hemerocallis*) are another easy-care choice for sunny slopes. Groundcovers such as bugleweed

(*Ajuga reptans*), pachysandra, and wild ginger (*Asarum canadense*) are good choices for slopes in light shade.

51 Fast-Growing, Moveable Screens

Hedges are often used to screen an area for privacy or to hide an ugly view. Unfortunately, even fast-growing hedge plants need three to four years to reach an effective size. But in a matter of weeks you can have a temporary screen using fast-growing herbaceous plants. When planted in a row of pots, they even make a moveable fence.

HOW TO DO IT
• Amaranths (*Amaranthus*), sunflowers (*Helianthus*), castor bean (*Ricinus communis*), and Mexican sunflower (*Tithonia rotundifolia*), all of which grow three to six feet tall, are good candidates for seasonal screens.

• Many ornamental grasses are perennials and will form a tall screen year after year (see Tip #52). Planted in pots they can be used as a portable hedge (see Tip #62).

52 Liven Up Fall With Ornamental Grasses

Great backdrop plants at the back of summer borders, ornamental grasses make emphatic visual statements in fall and winter when the garden lies dormant, and their seed heads look great in dried arrangements.

An Edible Screen

For a fast-growing hedge that's also edible, try Jerusalem artichoke, or sunchoke (*Helianthus tuberosus*). Pick out some plump unblemished tubers at the grocery store (they look like lumpy potatoes) and plant them shallowly in your garden where you want a screen or some shade. They quickly grow eight to ten feet tall, and in late summer, they are topped with yellow blossoms that look like miniature sunflowers. But be forewarned: Once planted, Jerusalem artichoke spreads.  No matter how diligent you are about harvesting the tubers, you won't get them all, and the stragglers will multiply. To harvest the edible tubers, dig into the soil at the base of the plant. You can do this in early fall, but the tubers will be more flavorful after a frost. If you mulch them with a foot of chopped leaves to keep the ground from freezing, you can harvest the cold-hardy tubers all through winter. Jerusalem artichokes can be boiled or baked but are best eaten raw—maybe with a sprinkle of salt or your favorite vegetable dip. They add a nutty crunch to salads.

Attractive focal points in the fall garden, ornamental grasses such as 'Karl Foerster' feather reed grass continue to provide structure to the landscape throughout the winter months.

HOW TO DO IT

• During autumn cleanup, leave ornamental grasses standing to become focal points in the garden in the winter. As the seed heads emerge in fall, the grasses turn from various shades of green and blue to beige, pink, and tan.

• The decorative seed heads are very attractive in dried winter bouquets. Cut the seed heads when they are beginning to emerge rather than when they are in full bloom, and hang them upside down to dry. Use them alone or mixed with other dried flowers and pods. The seed heads of northern sea oats (*Chasmanthium latifolium*) are particularly arresting, with clusters of chevronlike seeds that dangle from graceful arching stems like earrings.

53 Nurture a Self-Sown Garden

Among gardening's most delightful surprises are incidental flowers—volunteer plants that come up from seeds of a flower that you forgot to deadhead the previous year or from seed blown in by the wind or deposited by a bird after it passed through its digestive system. Encouraging self-seeders is an easy and inexpensive way to make your garden more serendipitous and floriferous.

HOW TO DO IT

• Set aside a corner of your yard for a self-sown garden. Plant it once with annuals that readily drop their seeds, and you'll never need replant.

• Keep an eye on the seedlings of self-sown flowers as they emerge in spring,

Planted once, salvias, snow-on-the-mountain, and spider flowers freely spread their seeds to create a new garden every year.

and thin them as needed to promote vigorous, unimpeded growth.

• Amaranths, spider flowers (*Cleome*), love-in-a-mist (*Nigella*), cosmos, cockscombs (*Celosia*), forget-me-nots (*Myosotis*), poppies (*Papaver*), and snow-on-the-mountain (*Euphorbia marginata*) are heavy self-seeders. Low-growing portulacas, impatiens, and ageratums will also come back yearly from dropped seeds.

54 Making a Moon Garden

Featuring mostly white flowers and silver-leafed plants, a moon garden is a wonderful place for a relaxing evening when it's too dark to appreciate the rest of the garden. In addition to its visual beauty, it has another dimension—fragrance, which is usually more pronounced after nightfall. There are lots of plant choices to brighten and perfume a moon garden from early spring to late fall, including annuals, perennials, bulbs, shrubs, and trees.

HOW TO DO IT

• To be able to fully appreciate a moon garden, locate it where you can see and smell it from up close. A spot under or near a window allows for viewing it from the house and catching the scent-filled night breezes. Or create a moon

Unwanted Volunteers

Volunteer plants can be welcome or not, depending on what they are and where they grow. There are annual poppies scattered all over my garden, and they are welcome. No matter how careful I am to harvest the pods without spilling any seeds, some escape, and the next year I find their bright flowers in surprising spots. Some years ago, a friend gave me some seedlings of scotch thistles (*Onopordum*) with the warning not to let their beautiful flowers go to seed. I forgot the warning and have been trying to get rid of volunteers ever since. Yes, it makes an impressive focal point, but I want to choose the focal points in my garden, not let the plant do it! Should self-sown plants get too pushy, deadhead more often and dispose of the spent flowers before they go to seed. Put them in a hot compost pile or dispose of them in the garbage.

garden close to a patio, a swimming pool, or another place that invites lingering on a hot summer night.

- Allow plenty of space between fragrant plants that flower at the same time to avoid conflicting aromas. Just as some colors clash, so do fragrances. If one of your plants has an especially strong perfume, give it some room.

- Select white-flowering plants that bloom at different times, and combine tall plants with shorter ones for a layered look: pansies (*Viola × wittrockiana*), hyacinths, and daffodils (*Narcissus*) in early spring; shasta daisy (*Leucanthemum × superbum*), lupines, peonies, and roses in early summer; feverfew (*Tanacetum parthenium*), four-o'clocks (*Mirabilis jalapa*), lilies, night phlox (*Zaluzianskya capensis*), petunias, white wild indigo (*Baptisia alba*), and moonflower (*Ipomoea alba*) in summer; boltonias, flowering tobaccos (*Nicotiana*), and angel's trumpets (*Datura,* syn. *Brugmansia*), the last two with sweet nighttime fragrance, in late summer and early fall.

- If space allows, include white-flowering shrubs in the moon garden, such as azaleas (*Rhododendron*) and rhododendrons, lilacs (*Syringa*), hydrangeas, mock oranges (*Philadelphus*), spireas (*Spiraea*), summersweet (*Clethra alnifolia*), and viburnums. Flowering trees for the moon garden are dogwoods (*Cornus*), stewartia, magnolias, crabapples (*Malus sylvestris* cultivars) and ornamental cherries (*Prunus* cultivars).

- Include some plants with white-shimmering foliage like lamb's ears (*Stachys byzantina*) and Russian sage (*Perovskia atriplicifolia*), which has silvery leaves and blue flowers.

- Plant a few aromatic herbs like rosemary (*Rosmarinus officinalis*) and thymes as well as scented geraniums (*Pelargonium* cultivars) among the white flowers and let them contribute their fragrances.

55 Easy Monochromatic Gardens

Combining shades and tones of the same color or limiting yourself to using a related group of colors is a fun way to create an exciting yet harmonious garden design. A predetermined palette can also make choosing plants easier.

HOW TO DO IT

- Create a blazing-hot garden by bringing together fiery reds, blinding yellows, and tropical oranges. To keep this hot theme under control, look for red-flowered cultivars of annuals and perennials that have a hint of yellow or orange in them.

- In a hot-themed design, don't limit yourself to vividly colored flowers; also look for plants with flashy leaves and seedpods like coleus and chiles (*Capsicum*).

A combination of pale flower colors and silvery foliage, this garden really glows after sunset.

Relying almost entirely on foliage for excitement, both of these monochromatic gardens use a variety of textures to add dimension. A chartreuse-themed garden of cannas, coleus, and ornamental grass (left) is a tropical knockout. Combining silver, gray, and blue foliage with subtle blue and lavender flowers, this garden (right) takes on a magical shimmer at dusk.

- Three of the most colorful plants can make a hot-palette garden all by themselves: coleus, crotons, and cannas. Add some scarlet sage (*Salvia splendens*) and a bunch of zinnias from the Sun Series, and you'll have a most unsubtle garden. Introduce some perennials like black-eyed Susans (*Rudbeckia*), coreopsis, goldenrods (*Solidago*), an assortment of hot-colored daylilies (*Hemerocallis*), yarrows (*Achillea*), and an edging of low-growing marigolds (*Tagetes*), and the garden will be even more fiery. In the fall the hot theme can be sustained with a collection of bright yellow and bronze chrysanthemums.

- The flip side of the hot monochromatic border is the cool-toned garden. It's just as full of color, but the cooler hues—think pinks, blues, and purples—are more subtle and have a calming effect. Many of the plants that have hot-colored cultivars also come in varieties with cool-colored flowers: zinnias, impatiens, pinks (*Dianthus*), geraniums (*Pelargonium*), and the stars of the fall garden, chrysanthemums. Petunias have so many color variations that they alone could make an attractive cool-color garden.

- To warm up a cool-themed garden featuring a lot of blues, mix in some reddish-blue flowers, such as *Ceanothus* 'Gentian Plume' and *Salvia* × *sylvestris* 'Montrose Best'.

- A subtle, elegant silver garden derives much of its magic from foliage colors. Plant choices include lamb's ears (*Stachys byzantina*), catnips (*Nepeta*), santolina, and wormwood (*Artemisia*). Try using an assortment of ornamental grasses, such as 'Heavy Metal' switch grass (*Panicum virgatum* 'Heavy Metal'), which adds a vertical element to the silver garden, and low-growing bulbous oat grass (*Arrhenatherum elatius* var. *bulbosum* 'Variegatum'), which prefers cool shade. Licorice plant (*Helichrysum petiolare*) is a silver-leafed plant that pulls the garden together as it spreads, covering the spaces between individual specimens.

- A monochromatic garden that takes center stage in low light is a white-flower or moon garden (see Tip #54).

- If you want to grow both cool- and hot-colored flowers in a small space, insert some white flowers and silver-leafed plants to create a transition between the two and avoid color clashes.

- A color wheel is a handy little gadget for helping you plan your garden palette. If two colors appear close to each other on the wheel, they will harmonize in the garden. If they are across from each other, they will provide high contrast. Combining too many plants with contrasting flower colors can easily give your garden a hodgepodge look.

The Accidental Garden

Sometimes gardens happen serendipitously. Some years ago, one of my sons gave me a blue spruce (*Picea pungens*) for my birthday. It was about 15 inches high and had beautiful color. Busy with fall chores I had no time to plant it so asked him to do it for me. "Just put it anyplace in the border where you see some vacant space," I said. The empty space he selected was smack in the middle of already dormant perennials. The following spring when the tree's new "candles" emerged, I sensed I had what nurserymen call a shiner, a blue spruce of outstanding color, a light blue and silver that was almost white.

Years later, as the tree began to dominate that section of the border, I realized that it was an outstanding focal point that would be even more attractive if the perennials around it echoed the silver and blue of its needles. From other parts of the garden I transplanted silver foliage plants to echo the color of the spruce. For a few touches of cool color I randomly placed a few clumps of lavender and catnip (*Nepeta*). The silver garden is especially attractive in the evening, turning almost luminescent after sunset.

Container Gardening

56 Container-Gardening Tips

Whether you are gardening on an acre or your front steps, you can grow flowers, herbs, vegetables, and even trees in containers. The planting and maintenance of a potted garden is a little different from gardening in the ground.

HOW TO DO IT

• Soil mixes: The secret to a successful potted garden is the quality of the soil. Don't use garden soil in your flower pots; it usually packs so tightly that it's difficult for roots to spread through its concretelike structure. Some of the best potting media aren't even true soil—commercial soil blends for container gardens are made up of a wide range of ingredients, the most common being peat moss, coir, vermiculite, perlite, sand, grit, compost, humus, and leaf mold, fortified with assorted nutrients. Free of soil-born pathogens, these mixes retain water yet drain easily, and their porosity encourages root growth. Some are formulated to be especially lightweight, which makes them useful for roof gardens.

• Pots: Of the many choices of container materials—wood, metal, cement, ceramic, glass—the most popular are clay and plastic. Clay is far more attractive than plastic, but it is porous and requires more frequent watering. A happy compromise are molded fiberglass containers that simulate expensive, decorative terra-cotta pots. Viewed from just a few feet away, it's hard to detect that these are faux clay rather than the real thing, and they retain moisture as well as plastic. Fiberglass is also lighter and more winter resistant than clay.

• Weight problems: No matter what they are made of, large pots filled with even the lightest soil mix are difficult

Before you hit the stores and get carried away by gorgeous displays, measure the pots of perennials that need to be transplanted and look for new pots with a diameter that's one to two inches larger.

Water evaporates fast through the porous walls of terra-cotta pots, making them ideal for drought-tolerant plants like sages. Moisture lovers like parsley need to be monitored carefully in clay pots.

to move. Here's a simple solution: Before filling the pot, line the bottom with empty aluminum cans or plastic bottles. Roots of herbaceous plants rarely need all the depth in an 18- or 24-inch pot, so the fillers are not depriving them of spreading space.

• Watering: In general, potted plants need to be watered more frequently than those growing in the ground. Watch the weather and water more frequently, even twice a day, on hot, windy days and less if it is cloudy and drizzly. Before watering, use the fingertip test: Insert your index finger into the container, and if the soil feels dry, water; if it's moist, don't.

• Fertilizing: When preparing the pots for planting, blend a generous pinch of slow-release fertilizer with the soil mix. Every other week, water plants with compost tea (see Tip #28) or with a liquid organic all-purpose fertilizer.

57 Great Plant Combos for Pots

The type, color, and texture of plantings set the tone of each container garden. It can be designed for a particular use, such as an herb or fragrance garden, or to meet certain conditions, such as dry or cold weather. Or it can be an eclectic mix of everything you love to grow, arranged in a mishmash of containers and plant combinations.

HOW TO DO IT

• Plants native to your region are an unexpected choice and often have the

Colorful annuals and herbs soften the edges of the stairs and make walking them a visual pleasure that can easily change from spring to fall with a rotating stock of plants.

added benefit of attracting local butterflies and hummingbirds.

- Try a variety of plants with colorful foliage but no flowers. Some of the most effective mixed plantings are those with analogous colors, such as purple, pink, and maroon or orange, yellow, and bronze.

- Mix and match: To create a classic arrangement for a big pot, plant a spiky, vertical element like *Dracaena* or fountain grass (*Pennisetum*) and surround it with a mix of shorter, colorful annuals along with some trailing plants.

- If regular watering is an issue, grow a cactus and succulent garden in containers. If you also want a lot of color,

look for bright-blooming but drought-tolerant, or xerophytic, plants such as butterfly weed (*Asclepias tuberosa*) and rose moss (*Portulaca* species).

58 Getting Creative With Containers

There are countless ways to create an appealing container-plant display. The effect can range from minimalist, by using simple, identical pots and filling them with one type or grouping of plants, to elaborate, with a variety of containers planted in a colorful tumble of flowers and foliage.

HOW TO DO IT

- Depending on the mood you want to achieve, plants can be potted in any-

Elevated in pots, short plants like basil and parsley command attention, are at a good height for smelling and picking, and—a nice touch for edibles—keep their foliage clean.

masonry supplies are sold, these heavy clay flues usually stand 24 inches high and vary from 8 to 18 inches square. An up-and-down skyscraper effect is more pleasing to the eye than having all the flues uniformly level: Vary their height by digging some into the soil at different depths and placing the rest at ground level.

• Reuse lithographed cans to make colorful, folksy pots. After you've finished a can of olive oil, coffee, or tomatoes, punch holes in the bottom for drainage and plant cottage-garden flowers or caladiums. For indoors, use them (without drainage holes) as cachepots for an assortment of potted herbs (see Tip #95).

thing from Grecian-style urns to old boots. But remember, good drainage is essential; unless you're growing plants that love wet feet, make sure the container has at least one drainage hole and sits on top of pot feet.

• For a formal look, use stone troughs, glazed earthenware pots, or classical vases arranged symmetrically, for example, on either side of an entranceway.

• "Found" planters like wooden washtubs and chipped teapots create a whimsical effect in an informal garden.

• Use window boxes and hanging pots where floor or ground space is limited.

• A good way to isolate aggressive plants or emphasize a group of flowers or herbs is to plant them in compost-filled chimney flues. Available where

59 Growing Herbs in Small Spaces

No room for an herb garden? Grow herbs in pots. A bunch of pots and a sunny terrace, sidewalk, or driveway are all you need. If you don't even have space to spread out the pots, think vertical: Arrange them on the steps of an old ladder, which takes up a meager square yard of space.

HOW TO DO IT

• For an instant potted garden: Buy small herbs in six-packs or two- to four-inch pots at your local nursery.

Maximize the potential of a small gardening space by going vertical. Be sure to reserve the most elevated spots for the plants that need the most light.

Transplant them into six- to eight-inch pots in a sterile soil mix that you have fortified with some mature compost. Water the plants well, keep them shaded for a couple of days to get them settled in their new homes, then move them to a spot where they get at least six hours of sunshine. Water when the top of the soil is dry to the touch. During hot, windy weather you may have to water every day, even twice a day.

- To save money: Annuals like dill (*Anethum graveolens*), basils (*Ocimum basilicum*) cilantro (*Coriandrum sativum*), and parsleys (*Petroselinum*), a biennial grown as an annual, are easy to start from seed. In early spring, fill pots with moistened soil mix and scatter seeds on the surface, barely cover them with a little more mix, and tamp down gently. Place the pots in plastic bags and move them to a sunny windowsill. When the seeds germinate, remove the bags. If all goes well, the seedlings will be pretty crowded. Harvesting begins soon after, by snipping out some plants where the seedlings grow thickest. When the herbs are a little more mature, use your fingers to further thin out weaker-looking plants, giving the remaining ones more room to grow. Move the plants outdoors as soon as it's warm enough.

- For a great harvest: Throughout the growing season, harvest herbs by pinching out the growing tips, which helps the plants grow bushier.

- Low-growing herbs elevated in chimney flues are easy to harvest when needed, and their assorted leaf shapes add another dimension to a corner of the garden (see Tip #58.

- For tips on growing herbs indoors, see Tip #68.

60 Mini-Vegetables for Containers

What could be better than to step outside your backdoor and gather your dinner fresh from a handy pot or hanging basket? An ever-growing variety of miniature vegetables suited for growing in containers makes it easy.

HOW TO DO IT

- Select a site that gets six to eight hours of full sunlight daily.

- Most vegetables need a lot of water, and they can dry out more quickly in containers than in the ground: To preserve moisture, pot plants in fiberglass or plastic containers instead of terra-cotta or wooden ones.

- Plant your mini-veggies in squat pots that are wider than high to help keep them from blowing over in summer storms.

- Look for some of the new miniature cultivars specially suited to container culture:

Tomatoes: The varieties 'Tiny Tim', 'Patio', 'Tumbler' were developed for pot culture.

Peppers: 'Sweet Pickle', a small bell pepper, and most chiles.

Keep a few pots of compact-growing chile peppers on a sunny windowsill for spicy harvests throughout the winter months.

Carrots: 'Parmex' or 'Thumbelina', both round varieties, don't need deep pots. 'Kinko', a stubby variety, grows to four inches.

Eggplants: Full-size varieties grow to 18 to 24 inches in a pot and need a large container and support. 'Bambino' is a "baby" hybrid that grows to 14 inches tall and produces one-inch dark purple fruits.

61 Overwintering Potted Plants

When it comes to surviving a freezing winter, container plants are at a disadvantage to those grown in the ground. The natural expansion and contraction of winter soil can cause pots to crack and the soil to heave, exposing the roots of container plants: Even plants hardy in frigid climates are vulnerable. You can take several steps to preserve your container garden until spring.

HOW TO DO IT

• Choose plants hardy to one to two zones colder than your region.

• Look for containers that can tolerate soil expansion due to freezing temperatures: For example, plastic, fiberglass, and wood are less prone to cracking than pottery or concrete.

• If possible, pot plants that remain outdoors year-round in oversize containers: The more soil there is to insulate the roots, the less likely they are to freeze.

• Once their leaves drop, cut hardy perennials that are to remain outdoors back to about five inches.

• To reduce heaving and root damage, heavily mulch containers with hay, chopped leaves, or shredded bark.

• Move terrace and rooftop containers to a sheltered spot out of the winter winds, preferably against a sunny wall or other structure. You can also cluster them and surround the group with bales of hay.

• To protect young potted trees and evergreens, surround them with a burlap screen.

• Before the first frost, move tropical plants into the house, and put half-hardy perennials in a cool garage or basement, where they will drop their leaves and go dormant. Don't forget about them, though: Keep them barely moist throughout the winter.

Identical pots of tall-growing foliage plants like summer cypress add elegant vertical interest to a flat garden space, and strategically placed, they also provide some privacy.

• Empty the soil from seasonal planters and store them upside down in a sheltered spot.

62 Making the Most of Portable Pots

Perhaps the best thing about container gardening is the fact that you can arrange and rearrange the plants for visual effect. You can also move your potted garden around to better accommodate space, watering, and light needs of particular plants.

HOW TO DO IT

• Pedestals and hanging baskets create vertical interest in the garden and can help guide the eye away from unsightly views. Line identical plantings, such as rosemary or summer cypress (*Bassia scoparia* f. *trichophylla,* syn. *Kochia trichophylla*), along a drive or pathway for a formal effect.

• Use container plants to mark a temporary path to guide guests from deck or patio to the yard. See Tip #51 for a moveable hedge of ornamental grasses.

Gardening Indoors

63 Make Your Cut Flowers Last

One of the nicest ways to enhance the ambiance of any room is with a vaseful of cut flowers. Chances are freshly cut flowers from your own garden will look nicer and last longer than store-bought ones, but no matter where they come from, here are ways to keep them going for as long as possible.

HOW TO DO IT

• Flowers from your garden should be gathered in early morning.

• When cutting spike flower stems such as snapdragons (*Antirrhinum majus*) and larkspur (*Consolida ajacis*), go for spikes with tight, barely opened buds, most of which will open when brought indoors.

• Cut flowers that grow on individual stems such as sunflowers (*Helianthus*) and pot marigold (*Calendula officinalis*) just as they fully open.

For long-lasting cut flowers, use a sharp knife, clippers, or shears—never scissors.

• Before arranging cut flowers, remove all leaves that would end up below the water line. Immediately place the stems in a bucket of room-temperature water. Make sure your vase is sparkling clean and free of any soapy residue. Cut all stems on a diagonal, and gently crush the tips of woody ones to facilitate water absorption.

Creating a dried flower arrangement is simple. All you need are the flowers, a few interesting seed heads, some florist's foam, and a container to put them in.

• Add a commercial preservative to the water, or make your own, following this simple recipe: To one quart of lukewarm water add one teaspoon sugar, one teaspoon household bleach, and two teaspoons lemon juice.

• The cooler the room that you keep your flower arrangement in, the longer it will last.

64 Dry Flowers for Winter Bouquets

You enjoy your flowers when they are growing out in the garden, so why not cut, dry, and assemble them into attractive arrangements to be savored throughout the winter?

HOW TO DO IT

• Flowers especially suited for drying include yarrows (*Achillea*), wormwoods (*Artemisia*), cockscomb (*Celosia argentea*), statice (*Limonium sinuatum*), strawflower (*Helichrysum bracteatum*), globe amaranth (*Gomphrena globosa*), and goldenrods (*Solidago*).

• Wild and ornamental grasses (see Tip #52) and weeds with attractive seed heads make nice companions. Look along roadsides for the seed heads of Queen Anne's lace (*Daucus carota*), common mullein (*Verbascum thapsus*), and seedpods of milkweeds (*Asclepias*).

• Cut flowers for drying just when the buds are beginning to open—at the latest just before they come into full bloom. Hang them upside down in a warm, dry spot and let them dry for about a month.

- Use florist's foam to anchor the flowers in your vase. Start with the tallest stems, then slowly add shorter ones around them. Let the size of the container determine the size of the bouquet. Constantly turn the arrangement and scrutinize it from different angles, adding or removing stems to keep the bouquet balanced.

- Use a toothpick to make a hole in the foam before you insert fragile stems. Replace or reinforce very weak stems, such as those of strawflower (*Bracteantha bracteata*), with thin wire.

- To make bouquets last, lightly spray them with hair spray.

65 Forcing Bulbs for Winter Bloom

What can be more cheerful in the dead of winter than a potful of flowering bulbs? With a little bit of planning you can have spring flowers in full bloom indoors months before they come up outside.

HOW TO DO IT

- Usually spring-flowering bulbs are planted outdoors in fall, and most bloom from March to May, depending on the type of plant. For bulbs to flower indoors in midwinter, they have to be tricked into spring mode with a period of cold. In cold-winter regions, plant the bulbs in pots in autumn and store them where the temperature is just above freezing—a mudroom or porch, garage, or unheated spare room will do nicely.

For much-welcomed winter flowers, store pots of bulbs in an unheated porch, mudroom, or garage, or in an improvised cold frame for eight to ten weeks, then bring them indoors to bloom.

Unlike other spring bulbs, paperwhite narcissus do not need a period of cold to bloom. Just put them in a bowl of potting mix or pebbles and add water until the bottom of each bulb is wet.

• Another option is to put them outside in a cold frame; a temporary one can be made with four straw bales arranged in a U-shape against a wall. Huddle the bulb pots close together, cover them with a foot of shredded leaves, and let nature do its work.

• In 12 weeks the bulbs will have filled the pots with roots, essential for the leaf and flower growth to come. Move the pots into the house. With 50°F to 70°F temperatures indoors and maybe some sunshine, you will have flowers in a few weeks. The cooler the room, the longer the flowers will last.

• Save the bulbs once the show is over and transplant them to the garden in spring, where they will bloom again the following year.

66 Paperwhite Narcissus: The Easiest Indoor Bulb

To fill your winter with flowers and fragrance, nothing is easier than growing paperwhite (*Narcissus tazetta*) bulbs.

HOW TO DO IT

• Pick a watertight bowl that's wide and deep enough to hold at least a dozen bulbs and fill it with three to six inches of soil mix, marbles, pebbles, or gravel. Make a one-inch depression in the growing medium for each bulb and place them so close so that they touch. The idea is to wind up with a crowded but impressive bouquet.

• Next, add enough water to the bowl so that the bottom of each bulb is wet. Depending on the temperature of the room, you'll have fragrant blos-

Encircle tall-growing paperwhites with a strand of yarn to keep them upright as they blossom.

soms in four to six weeks; the warmer the room, the sooner the blooms. But once they bloom, the flowers will last longer in a cool room.

• As the paperwhites near maturity, some varieties' tall, slender flower stems and leaves have a tendency to topple over. Forestall this by encircling the leaves and flower stems with a decorative piece of yarn or ribbon to keep them upright as they bloom.

• If you want paperwhites in bloom throughout the winter months, buy a good supply in the fall when they are readily available at garden centers and mail-order nurseries; if you wait until December, many sources will be sold out. For nonstop bloom, start a new pot every two or three weeks. To accelerate growth, move the pots to a warm, bright spot; to slow growth, keep them dark and cool.

• Unlike forced tulips, daffodils, and hyacinths, paperwhites cannot be saved and planted out in the garden to bloom again the following year. Treat them as annuals and compost them after they have bloomed.

67 Harvest Veggies From Your Windowsill

One of the great moments of home gardening is picking that first red-ripe tomato in early July and eating it—sun warmed—out in the garden. Fast-forward to cold but bright January and

a pot of 'Tiny Tim' tomatoes, loaded with fruit, right on your windowsill. Eating the first ripe 'Tiny Tim'—small as it is—is almost as gratifying as biting into that first tomato in summer. Not every vegetable can be grown indoors in the average house or apartment, but many can.

HOW TO DO IT

• Think positive but workable: Forget about growing the big stuff like corn, squashes, melons, and pumpkins; root crops are possible but impractical; and don't even think about pole beans. However, though it's hard to grow conventional full-size tomatoes, peppers, and eggplants inside, there are miniature versions, such as small determinate tomatoes like 'Tiny Tim' and 'Patio', that can do well given enough light and warmth (see Tip #60).

- Salad greens, which require less sunlight and can grow in cooler rooms, are often successful indoors when other vegetables fail to flourish.

- To add some mild onion flavor to winter salads, grow chives, which thrive indoors (although they need to be exposed to freezing weather for a about a month of dormancy before being brought indoors).

- Most herbs can be grown successfully indoors (see Tip #68).

- Compact pepper plants such as *Capsicum annum* 'Gypsy' or 'Sweet Pickle' will add zest to your salad bowl, as will small chiles such as 'Chilly Chili' and 'Medusa'—both of which are solidly covered with tiny red, yellow, and orange peppers.

- When you're ready to plant your indoor garden, use big pots so the roots have as much room as possible to grow. Use equal quantities of compost and potting mix. Plant the seeds, and once they're growing vigorously, snip out all but two or three of the strongest plants. Water as needed using the fingertip test: Stick your index finger in the soil, and if it comes up dry, water; if it's damp, don't (see Tips #44 and #45).

- The most important element for growing vegetables indoors is sunlight—as much as you can find in your house. For example, a south-facing bay window that gets additional light from the east and west is an ideal place for a winter garden. Lacking that, smaller south- and west-facing windows upstairs can also support indoor vegetables if they get at least four to six hours of sunlight a day. Consider keeping tomato pots in a south window until about two in the afternoon, then move them to a west window for the rest of the day. Peppers and eggplants have the same need for sun as tomatoes. Salad greens and herbs can get by with less sunshine, but they still require bright light.

- Every other week, give your indoor vegetables a boost with an organic liquid fertilizer.

- One if the pluses of winter indoor gardening is the absence of hungry critters, such as squirrels, rabbits, deer,

Edible gardening indoors calls for growing compact varieties, such as 'Tiny Tim' tomatoes.

For fresh parsley all winter long, sow some seeds in buried containers a month or two before the first fall frost, and transfer the potted plants to a sunny spot indoors.

and groundhogs. But there are tiny predators. To control aphids and whiteflies, place each container in the kitchen sink every two weeks and spray the entire plant with lukewarm water. The spray should have enough force to dislodge any bugs and wash them down the drain.

68 Fresh-Picked Herbs Year-Round

Early spring is not the only time for starting an herb garden, and the great outdoors is not the only place where it can thrive. Just don't expect bumper harvests from a windowsill garden, especially in winter, because herbs grown in winter on even the sunniest of windowsills receive fewer hours of sunlight than those grown outside in

the summer garden. Nevertheless, you should always be able to harvest enough to make the indoor herb garden worth your while.

• You can start annual herbs such as basil, chervil, and dill from seed anytime of year indoors.

• To get a head start on an indoor herb garden, acquire a few starter plants of annual herbs or perennials such as sages and varieties of mint.

• Unless you have an atrium or greenhouse with lots of room and plenty of light, avoid trying to grow large herbs like lovage and angelica.

• Start parsley from seed in August in pots sunk in the garden to get a jump on your winter garden. (You can't just dig up a clump that was growing in the garden all summer because parsley's long taproot makes it difficult to transplant.) Fill four-inch clay pots with a compost, sand, and peat-moss mix. Sink the pots into the ground until the rims barely show. Scatter a pinch of parsley seeds over the surface, barely cover with soil, then water. Once the seeds have sprouted and are one to two inches high, snip out all but three to five of the sturdiest plants with scissors. A few weeks before the projected first frost date, dig up the pots, clean them, and move them into the house. Grow the parsley plants in a sunny window.

69 Overwintering Tender Perennial Herbs

Warmth-loving herbs such as rosemary (*Rosmarinus officinalis*), bay (*Laurus*

nobilis), lemon grass (*Cymbopogon citratus*), and lemon verbena (*Aloysia triphylla*) thrive in summer gardens. But with the exception of some hardy rosemary varieties, these tender perennials will not survive when temperatures dip down to the freezing mark or below. However, you can bring all four herbs indoors to spice up your winter cuisine.

HOW TO DO IT

• About three weeks before the first projected frost date, dig up the herb plant with a generous ball of soil clinging to the roots. Take a clay flowerpot with a diameter two inches larger then the root ball and place an inch of gravel and a couple of inches of compost in the bottom. Insert the herb, fill the space between the pot and the root ball with more compost, tamp down gently to get rid of air pockets, then water. Leave the freshly potted herb outdoors in the shade for about a week. Before moving the pot indoors, hose off the foliage to dislodge any bugs and let it dry off.

• All four herbs will live through the winter indoors with limited sunshine, but they do best on a sunny windowsill.

• Water when the top inch of soil is dry, and apply a liquid organic fertilizer a couple of times during the winter.

It's not necessary to buy new plants of tender herbs such as rosemary and bay every year in cool climates. Overwintering them indoors (left) not only saves you money but also provides you with fresh herbs all winter long. Pot up garden herbs a few weeks before frost (right).

Poinsettias often come wrapped in foil. Cut a hole in the bottom so water doesn't drown the plant.

• Around the time when you plant tomatoes, move the tender herbs outdoors again, first letting them harden off in a sheltered spot out of the sun for about a week.

70 Safe and Easy Pest Control

One of the best insecticides for houseplants is plain water. And as you blast the bugs, you benefit the plant in two more ways: You rid it of dust that collects on the leaves and keeps the plant from absorbing the maximum amount of light, and you give it a much-needed drink—a special bonus in most homes during the winter heating season.

HOW TO DO IT

• Fill a cleaned-out pump-spray bottle with water, preferably distilled; place a bug-infested houseplant in the kitchen sink or bathtub; then thoroughly douse it with the spray bottle. Lay the plant on its side and rotate it as you spray to ensure that the jets of water reach the undersides of the leaves to dislodge any aphids, spider mites, and whiteflies.

71 Make Your Poinsettias Last

In the right spot, this traditional Christmas plant will remain bright and colorful until early April. Poinsettia "flowers" last so long because they are not really flowers at all but bracts, or modified leaves, much like those of dogwoods. The true flower of the poinsettia is the group of tiny yellow beads in the center of each cluster of bracts,

When the heat is on, houseplants benefit from sitting in a humidity tray of moistened pebbles.

which in addition to the traditional red, now come in pink, white, yellow, and even a polka-dot variety.

HOW TO DO IT

• Keep poinsettias in a cool, bright room out of direct sunlight and drafts. They last longest with temperatures no higher than 70°F in the daytime and 55° to 60°F at night.

• Poinsettias need to be watered often when in flower. They also benefit from adequate humidity. Keep an open bottle of water nearby, or set the plant on a humidity tray (see Tip #72).

72 The Best Way to Water Houseplants

Watering houseplants is a whole different ballgame from watering plants in the garden outdoors. Did you know that more houseplants are killed from too much rather than too little water? Here are a few ways to make sure your indoor plants get just enough moisture—but no more.

HOW TO DO IT

• Before watering houseplants, use the fingertip test: Insert your index finger in the top half inch of soil. If it feels dry to the touch, water; if it's even slightly moist, don't. Another good trick is the heft test. If the pot feels light, it could use some water. If it is heavy, wait a few days before you water.

• For houseplants, humidity is almost as important as irrigation. Most homes are dry during the heating

Plants in glazed pots (foreground), retain moisture better than unglazed clay ones (background); cluster them to boost humidity.

season—not an ideal environment for houseplants, many of which come from humid tropical climates. Clustering plants closely together helps boost humidity slightly. Even better, keep your indoor plants in a tray over a layer of wet pebbles. As the water, which should not quite reach the top of the pebbles, evaporates, the plants receive some beneficial humidity. But be sure that the pots don't sit in the water; few plants can tolerate soggy feet.

73 How to Water While You're on Vacation

All houseplant lovers face a common problem—how to keep their plants from drying out while they're away from home. Here are some ideas for keeping plants moist for a week or longer.

HOW TO DO IT

• Saturate the soil of your potted plants. Place each plant in a plastic bag punctured with a few holes and seal it with a twist tie. Put them all in the bathtub or in a large plastic tub, and have a nice vacation.

• Ball up sheets of newspaper, soak them in water, and stuff them around watered plants clustered in the sink or bathtub, out of the sun and away from heat. The wet paper keeps the air around the plants humid.

Water-soaked balls of newspaper nestled around potted plants in the sink will keep the surrounding air humidified while you're away.

Vegetable Gardening

74 Weed-Free Asparagus Beds

Older asparagus beds have a tendency to get weedy. If you apply a thick layer of mulch right after the spears break through the soil early in the growing season, you can eliminate weeds in an earth-friendly and back-saving way. The few weeds that aren't smothered by the mulch are easy to pull out by hand.

HOW TO DO IT

• If you have a lushly growing lawn, it will probably need mowing right around the time the asparagus spears emerge. Use the grass clippings to mulch the bed. Before applying them, though, empty the collected grass on either side of the asparagus bed or spread it out on a hard surface to dry; if you pile the fresh grass on the bed immediately, it will become a slimy,

moldy, smelly mess. To make the grass dry faster, turn it over every few hours. After a sunny day or two, it will be ready to spread. Repeat the process as you continue mowing, piling dried clippings on the bed until you have a thick layer. At the end of

Pesticide-free lawn clippings are a great free source of mulch in the asparagus patch and elsewhere in your edible garden.

Eliminating Asparagus Beetles

As the asparagus harvests cease toward the end of June, the spears elongate and grow tall and produce delicate, ferny leaves that are the favorite food of the asparagus beetle. The small black larvae can completely denude the foliage, which the plants need to nourish next year's spears. Vigorously shake the ferny stems to dislodge the larvae before they develop into beetles. Once they've dropped onto the mulch, they cannot climb back up the asparagus stems.

the season, the grass mulch will have decomposed into a nutritious, rich compost.

• If grass clippings aren't available, apply a thick layer of another organic mulch as soon as the spears have broken through the ground.

75 Harvest Beans All Summer Long

With staggered plantings and a few other clever tactics you can harvest succulent tender beans in manageable quantities from your vegetable garden for months on end and fill in the sea-

son with a succession of spring and autumn crops to boot.

HOW TO DO IT

• Plant short rows of beans at frequent intervals to keep harvests small but stretched out over the entire growing season. This avoids the feast-or-famine phenomenon—lots of beans all at once, then nothing.

• For maximum yields from small spaces, plant bush beans in double rows one foot apart, spacing seeds four inches apart in the rows. As the plants grow, they will support each other and shade out most weeds.

• For the best flavor and to keep the plants productive, pick beans often, while the pods are small and skinny.

76 Making More Broccoli

Broccoli, a hardy, cool-weather vegetable that can take temperatures down to the mid-20s, should be planted in most areas in early spring or late summer. If you plant out seedlings in late summer, they still have lots of time to

Succession planting is a fancy term for starting a few rows of beans or other vegetable every week or so for a long, continuous harvest.

develop a heavy root system and make good top growth before cool weather slows them down.

HOW TO DO IT

- As they near maturity, broccoli tops grow big and fat. After harvesting the big central head, don't pull up and compost the plant—below where the central head was cut, many smaller heads will sprout from each leaf node. Your chances of getting a second harvest are better in the fall.

- As temperatures warm up in spring, broccoli tends to bolt. The tight green heads open up and develop pretty yellow flowers, which are edible. Trim them off and add to mixed salads, sprinkle them on soup, or use them as a garnish for main dishes. They are also attractive in floral bouquets.

Like all plants in the cabbage family, broccoli grows best in soft, fertile soil in slightly raised beds. Add lots of compost to the soil.

77 Increasing Your Corn Crop

Ever wonder why some or most of the kernels are missing in some ears of corn? That means the corn hasn't been pollinated properly. The tassels that form atop corn plants produce pollen, which is carried by the wind to the fine strands of silk that emerge lower on the stalk. Every strand of silk is connected to a potential corn kernel. If no pollen falls on a strand of silk, its kernel won't develop. This is more apt to happen when the corn is grown in long rows. You can greatly improve chances of pollination by planting your corn patch appropriately.

Pollen needs to reach each strand of silk in order for all the kernels in an ear of corn to properly develop.

HOW TO DO IT

- Plant corn in blocks of four to six short rows rather than one or two long, single-file rows.

- For optimum pollination, your corn patch should measure at least four feet by four feet. This also applies if you decide to plant corn with pumpkin (see Tip #78).

- For top yields from the corn patch, space plants six to eight inches apart in rows about a foot and a half apart. When the plants are eight to ten inches high, side-dress with a balanced organic fertilizer. Sprinkle the fertilizer six inches from the plants and water it in.

- To extend the length of your corn harvest, make successive plantings every two to three weeks through the beginning of summer as space allows.

78 Interplanting Corn and Pumpkin to Save Space

Many gardeners are reluctant to plant sweet corn because it occupies too much space in their garden for too long. For the same reason, they avoid planting pumpkins or winter squash. However, by planting them in close proximity to each other, you can have crops of both in the space of one.

HOW TO DO IT

- Plant the pumpkin seeds first, point down, five to six seeds to a hill, with ten feet between hills. After the seeds germinate, in about ten days, pinch out all but three plants per hill. (For more on planting pumpkin seeds, see Tip #80.)

- When the pumpkin seedlings show three to four leaves, plant the corn. Set out three to four seeds in a cluster spaced eight to ten inches apart in rows two feet apart. If you were to plant them at the same time, the faster-growing corn would shade the pumpkin seedlings and stunt their growth. In their infancy, the pumpkin plants need lots of warmth and sunshine to get them off to a good start. As both grow, the corn eventually will shade the spreading pumpkin vines. At this stage of their growth the pumpkins can use the shade, which helps conserve moisture needed to produce full-size fruits. Still later, after the corn is harvested and the stalks

Save space by planting corn and pumpkin or squash together. Add beans and you have the "three sisters" of Native American plantings.

Vegetable and flower seedlings can be set out in the garden earlier than recommended if they are protected from the cold. Use bottomless plastic milk jugs or wire cages wrapped with plastic to fashion temporary greenhouses.

begin to dry, the pumpkins will again receive the ample sunshine necessary for their ripening and curing.

- See Tip #77 for hints on aiding corn pollination.

- If you'd like to try the "three sisters" approach, plant four to eight bean seeds around the corn plants when they are six inches tall. The beans will wind their way up the growing cornstalks, which will serve as their supports. Being legumes, the beans will replenish the soil with nitrogen as they grow. Native Americans often planted a fish with the pumpkin seed to give the growing plants a nutritional boost.

79 Temporary Greenhouses for Seedlings

To get a head start on the growing season, protect cold-sensitive vegetable seedlings like tomatoes, peppers, and eggplants, as well as flowering annual and tender perennial seedlings, in spring by covering them with a homemade plastic barrier. The vegetables will yield fruit a week or two sooner than unprotected plants, and the flowers will begin blooming earlier.

HOW TO DO IT
- Make cylinders out of chicken wire large enough to cover the plants and allow for some growth while the plants still need coddling from the cold.

You can get a head start on vegetables that require a long growing season by planting them early after warming the soil.

- Cover the sides and the tops of the cylinders with plastic, using string to secure the plastic to the chicken wire. To prevent winds from toppling over the miniature greenhouses, tie each to a sturdy stake driven into the ground.

- Place the greenhouses over the tender plants as soon as they are transplanted. When the days get warmer, remove the protective covers during the day and replace them about an hour before sunset.

- If the weather turns unusually cold, invert a big cardboard box over the greenhouses.

- Once the ground has warmed, add an organic mulch—straw, grass clippings, chopped leaves—to retain the warmth and smother weeds. When the danger of frost has passed, remove the temporary greenhouses.

80 Getting a Bumper Crop of Long-Season Veggies

For a bumper crop of vegetables such as pumpkins, winter squashes, and melons, which require a long growing season and need warm soil and lots of sunshine, plant them as early as possible by warming up the soil yourself.

HOW TO DO IT

- Around the last frost date, dig a hole 18 inches deep and across and fill the bottom half with compost. Next, fill the balance of the hole with a mix of

sand, compost, and garden soil. Top it with more soil to make a six-inch mound, water, then cover the hill with black plastic. Let the mound heat up for about ten days.

- Cover the surrounding area with a mulch of leaves, dried and pesticide-free grass clippings, or straw.

- Cut a slit in the plastic and plant six seeds a few inches apart, then water. Cover the seeds with a bottomless plastic milk jug to heat up the soil even more. Remove the jug when the seeds germinate.

- When the seedlings are three inches high, pinch out all but two of the sturdiest ones and remove the plastic from the mound. Water the spreading plants weekly if there is no rain. As the weather gets hot, the jump-started vines will spread quickly, flower, and form fruit that grow larger with each passing day.

- As the melons start to ripen, pick them up off the soil and rest them on bottomless coffee cans to speed ripening and prevent rotting.

- When the stems easily pop off, the melons are ready to pick. Pumpkins are ready to harvest when they are fully colored. Squashes are ripe when they attain their full size. To harvest, cut, don't pull, to separate the fruits from their vines.

- To toughen their skins, cure the fruits for three weeks in a hot, dry spot, then store them in a cool place. They will keep all winter.

81 Double Your Harvest With Intercropping

Intercropping, or interplanting, is growing two or more plants in the same area in the garden. By intercropping you can fit many more vegetables into a small garden space. The idea is to plant fast-growing crops in open spaces between slower-growing vegetables, and to combine cool-season vegetables with warm-season vegetables in the same plot.

HOW TO DO IT

- A classic combination is fast-growing lettuce planted between rows of slower-growing broccoli or cabbage. By the time the broccoli and cabbage need their full 18 inches of space, the lettuce will have been picked and eaten. It's easiest to use started lettuce seedlings, but a pinch of lettuce seed scattered in the spaces between the broccoli or cabbages will also work. When seeded lettuce is firmly rooted, pinch or snip out all but the strongest plants.

- Plant warm-weather crops like beans and tomatoes between cool-weather crops such as salad greens, peas, and radishes. The cool-weather plants are harvested as the warm-weather crops continue to grow and mature.

- As the growing season begins to wane, plant cool-weather vegetables between the warm-weather plants, which will provide much-needed shade for the germinating seeds and developing plants. Take out the warm-weather crops as they pass their peak to make room for the cool-weather vegetables.

Quick-growing cool-season lettuce will have been harvested by the time its space is shaded out by slower-growing cabbage and broccoli.

Even cool-climate gardeners can have a wide range of fresh vegetables well into autumn: This tasty and colorful multicultural late-season garden features French celeriac, ferny-leafed Italian finocchio, ruby Swiss chard, Japanese mizuna, Italian radicchio, and American 'Salad Bowl' lettuce.

82 Hardy Vegetables for the Late-Season Garden

Too many vegetable growers overlook the potential for keeping the garden going at the end of the season. Yet the soil is warm, ideal for germinating seeds and getting plants off to a good start. Warm days and cool nights are made to order for members of the cabbage family, the many salad greens, and most root crops. These hardy, or cool-weather, vegetables thrive in the cooler months of the year and can even take light frosts and temperatures down to the mid-20s.

HOW TO DO IT

- The key to a productive garden of hardy late-season vegetables is knowing the average first frost date in your area. Check the days to maturity on the seed packet and count back that number from the first frost date to determine the last day that these seeds could be planted and still produce edibles. Bear in mind, however, that even as the vegetables mature, cool weather will be fast approaching—and potentially curtailing your harvest time unless you plant crops that are hardy enough to withstand cooling temperatures and perhaps even frosts.

- Forget about new plantings of tender—or warm-weather—crops in the late-season garden, such as tomatoes, peppers, eggplants, squashes, corn, and beans. The days and especially the nights are not warm enough, and there will not be enough time for them to mature before they are withered by the cold. Having said that, in early August, I sometimes plant what I call a Russian roulette crop of, say, 50-day beans or zucchini in my New Jersey garden. If frost comes late and there's a warm Indian summer, I harvest in October. If frost comes early, the beans and zucchinis are no more. But there are still the leafy greens, root vegetables, and cabbage relatives that thrive in the cool weather, and the garden will continue to yield these tasty vegetables well into the colder season.

- For advice on extending the season by using row covers and mulches to protect tender and hardy vegetables against the cold, see Tip #83.

83 Protecting Vegetables From Late-Season Cold

With a bit of preparation, I can continue harvesting vegetables from my New Jersey garden in October, November, and even December. The trick is to cover the crops to protect them from the potentially killing cold. Cover tender vegetables, such as tomatoes, peppers, eggplants, summer squashes, and cucumbers before the first frost. Warm-weather veggies will continue to grow into late fall, but don't expect the same vigorous growth and abundant harvests you had in mid-season. Nonetheless, even if the beans are less productive and the tomatoes a little less tasty, the harvests are welcome. When sustained cold descends, cover hardy vegetables to extend their season. The following devices will shield your plants from frost and offer some protection from temperatures down to the high 20s; beyond that, the

Hardy and Tender Vegetables: Telling the Difference

For gardeners new to vegetable growing, the jargon can be baffling. Two words to be on familiar terms with are "hardy" and "tender." These don't refer to how chewy the vegetables are, or whether they are soft or al dente to the bite, but rather how much cold the plants can tolerate. An easy way to distinguish between hardy and tender vegetables is to consider which part is edible. Vegetables that develop from flowers, technically fruits, are generally tender and should be planted after all danger of frost has passed. In this group are tomatoes, cucumbers, okra, squashes, melons, pumpkins, peppers, eggplants, and beans. There are two exceptions, however: peas and fava beans, which are cold hardy and grow best when planted early.

Vegetables that do best in cooler weather are root crops like beets, carrots, and parsnips; all the salad greens, including lettuces; and members of the cabbage family like broccoli, cauliflower, red and green cabbages, and especially kale, collards, and Brussels sprouts, whose flavors are enhanced when the plants are touched by frost. Plant all these hardy vegetables early in the season and again in summer for late-season harvest.

Covering vegetables early and late in the season to protect them from frost can extend your harvest two months or even more, depending on where you live.

vegetables will freeze even with protection. But by then you will have gotten an extra two months or so of eating fresh from the garden.

HOW TO DO IT

- Side-dress hardy vegetables as the warm season wanes with a thick layer of straw, leaves, or another organic mulch to help keep the soil warm.

- One economical plant protector that's especially good for tiny heads of lettuce is a bottomless one-gallon milk jug placed over each plant.

- To protect a wide row planting, arch a sheet of translucent corrugated fiberglass over the greens and block the ends with smaller sections of the same.

- An easy, high-tech way to protect vegetables is with floating row covers. They are made with materials so lightweight—such as Reemay fabric—that they need to be anchored to keep them from blowing away. You can use stones for this purpose or wire coat hangers cut up and bent into six-inch U-shaped "hairpins."

- A money-saving approach is to use plastic shower curtains or drop cloths to cover your crops. Unlike the special fabric of commercial covers, they are too heavy to "float" atop the plants, hence you'll need to create a frame. One way is to bend wire fencing with a two-by-four-inch mesh into half cylinders and invert them

Garlic—as well as shallots and onions—can be started in a sunny windowsill indoors if the weather doesn't permit early planting out in the garden.

over your vegetables, and cover the fencing with your choice of plastic covering. The plants beneath are sheltered from the first frost and even protracted cold. An additional benefit: If you install the wire cages early in the season, they protect the vegetables from voracious deer and rodents. (To keep hungry intruders from wiggling under at the ends of the rows, cover the openings with chicken wire.)

84 Jump-Starting Onions, Shallots, and Garlic

To get big fat bulbs of garlic, onions, and shallots, the earlier sets are planted, the better. But in some regions, the weather is often wet and rainy in early spring, making early planting difficult or impossible. If that's the case for you, consider starting these alliums indoors.

HOW TO DO IT

• Step 1: Plant the edible allium sets indoors in plastic compartmented trays (the kind that nursery-started plants come in) one month before you can safely plant cool-season vegetables in the garden.

• Step 2: Fill the trays with a moistened mix of equal parts compost and peat moss. Gently push a garlic clove, shal-

How to Select Onion Sets

When buying onion sets, look for the smallest sets available—dime size or smaller. There are twice as many small sets to the pound, so you save money. Small sets are also less likely to send up flower stalks, spending their energy instead on forming fat bulbs, which is what you want. If you do notice a flower stalk developing in the leaf cluster—it is typically rounder and more rigid than the leaves—pinch it out before it grows more than an inch or two high. If the flower stalk is allowed to mature, the onion will only store for a short time.

Shallots: The Prolific Allium

Sixty shallot bulbs planted in five rows, a dozen bulbs in each row, will yield between 500 and 600 nice big shallots at harvest time. Unlike an onion set, which will produce just one onion at maturity, a single shallot bulb will divide and produce from six to ten, sometimes even a dozen new bulbs.

lot, or onion halfway into the mix in each compartment.

• Step 3: Place the trays on a sunlit, sheltered porch or in a south-facing window of the house.

• Step 4: Water the sprouting bulbs as needed to keep the soil moist. In three or four weeks, a solid mass of roots will fill the cells and the green tops will have grown two to four inches.

• Step 5: When the weather permits, harden off the plants in a sheltered spot outdoors for a few days, then

plant them in the garden six to eight inches apart in rows spaced about ten inches apart.

• See Tip #86 for another way to give alliums a head start.

85 Grow Shallots in Raised Beds

As most cooks know, the wonderful, delicate flavor of shallots lends itself to classic dishes and spontaneous creations alike. The cost of store-bought shallots inspires frugality, but if you grow your own in raised beds, you can use them lavishly.

HOW TO DO IT

• To maximize their yield, grow shallots in raised beds enriched with lots of compost and fortified with a high-nitrogen organic fertilizer balanced with wood ashes, which contain lots of phosphorus and potassium.

• Let your prepped bed sit for a week to give the nutrients time to sink in and weed seeds time to germinate. Rake the bed again to stir up the weed seedlings, which will then wither away in the sun.

Why shallots sell for several dollars a pound is baffling, because they are one of the easiest vegetables to grow, especially in raised beds. And for the space they occupy—rows need only be eight inches apart—their yield is remarkable.

- To make straight rows, use string to stake out two parallel lines spaced about eight inches apart. Plant the first row, making holes eight inches apart with your finger just deep enough to barely cover each shallot (place bulbs pointed tip up). After planting the first row, take up the first line of string and move it over eight inches to keep the second row parallel with the first, and so on.

- Immediately after planting all the rows, water the sets in. Shallots need an inch of water weekly—more if the weather is sunny and windy. Though they certainly do not like poor drainage, be sure to water the shallots if it fails to rain regularly.

- Fertilize the plants with fish emulsion or another liquid organic fertilizer every three to four weeks until about a month before harvest time.

- Harvest the shallots when the green tops start to flop over and begin to turn tan. Cure the bulbs in a warm, dry place for about a week before storing them.

86 Late-Season Planting of Alliums

In most climates, starting alliums late in the season and overwintering them outdoors is better than putting them in early in the spring (see Tip #84). This gives the bulbs' root systems plenty of time to develop before they go dormant in winter, which benefit from the early rains that would only delay spring planting. And planting alliums in the fall frees up time for other spring chores.

Braiding Garlic and Shallots for Easy Storage

I like to plait garlic and shallots for storage, so I dig up the bulbs when the tops are more green than tan. If they are too dry, the foliage crumbles and breaks too

easily to be braided. To give more strength to the braid, I weave in a doubled-over length of sturdy string with the green stems; this also provides a handy loop for hanging the garlic or shallot braid. Divide the stems into three clusters of leaves, one vertical, the others forming an X over the center cluster; then crisscross the leaves, weaving in the supporting string as you go so it becomes part of the plait. As you get near the top of the leaves, add more bulbs to lengthen the braid.

HOW TO DO IT

- Turn over the soil in the bed where you want to plant onions, garlic, or shallots and work in some compost, aged manure, or leaf mold—these plants flourish in rich, loose soils.

- Plant as soon as the soil temperature has cooled to around 60°F and the first hard frost is about six weeks away.

- Use your finger to make a hole in the soil, and push the onion set or garlic clove into the soil, pointed tip straight up, so that it is covered with about 1½ inches of soil. See Tip #85 for advice on growing shallots.

- Once you see a row of bright green slender stalks in spring, dust the beds with wood ashes on a day when there is rain in the forecast. This should aid the plants' vigor.

87 Supporting Peas

One of the joys of growing your own vegetables is the unmatched flavor of just-picked peas. The vines are best grown off the ground, but this makes picking convenient—maybe too convenient. For anyone going into the garden, the clean, fat pods hanging on the vines are just begging to be eaten on the spot, making it hard to gather enough peas to make it to the dinner table, no matter how sizable the planting.

HOW TO DO IT

- To support tall-growing sugar snap peas as well as conventional peas, build a sturdy, five-foot-high fence of brush that will support the upward growth of the plants: Stretch a string line to mark a straight row. Then, at each end of the row, simply push a twiggy branch from a spring-pruned tree or shrub vertically into the soft garden soil. Fill in the fence with more branches, weaving and overlapping side twigs. When you're done, remove the string.

- Five-foot-tall tomato cages are easily installed and can support several pea plants each.

- String rows of baling twine a foot apart horizontally on saplings or bamboo poles spaced 18 to 24 inches apart, or make a fence of concrete reinforcing wire (available in five-by-

Branches culled from pruning trees and bushes in your garden can be used to create a rustic fence for supporting peas.

Bounty from the garden picked just before a deep freeze doesn't have to be immediately canned or frozen. Many vegetables will keep in cool, dry storage for weeks or even months.

ten-foot sections), held up vertically with rebar or steel rods.

• Plant peas close to the pea supports on both sides. Water immediately after planting and weekly thereafter.

• As the peas grow, their tendrils will twirl around the branches, pulling the plants upward. As the peas mature and the pods fatten, pick them frequently. Most varieties will keep producing until the weather gets hot.

• When it's time to set out tomato seedlings (just after the last frost date in cooler zones), transplant them among the mature pea vines. After the peas finish bearing, prune the vines off at ground level to give the tomatoes full advantage of the space and supports—with the added bonus of nitrogen that the peas have fixed in the soil.

88 Storing Hardy Vegetables

Canning and freezing are good ways to preserve the edibles you grow in your garden, but both are quite labor-intensive. Dry storage is much easier and suitable for vegetables such as pumpkins, winter squashes, potatoes, shell beans, cabbages, carrots, beets, Jerusalem artichokes, onions, shallots, and garlic, as well as herbs, apples, and pears—plenty of ingredients with which to create a wide variety of winter meals.

HOW TO DO IT

• Handle winter squashes and pumpkins carefully when harvesting to avoid bruising. After cutting them off the vines, leaving on a two- to four-inch stem, let them cure out in the sun for about a week to toughen their rinds, then move them inside to a place where it's dry and above freezing, such as a garage, attic, or sheltered porch.

• Spread onions, shallots, and garlic in a shady cool spot after harvesting. Once their papery skins are dry, trim the roots and foliage and store them in a cool, dry place. Or braid them and hang them to dry in a cool place (see box on page 99).

• Bunch herbs and hang them upside down by their stems to dry. Or place them in brown paper bags, label, and store them in the refrigerator.

- Keep potatoes where it is dark and temperatures are just above freezing or in the low 40s. Bring cold-stored potatoes to room temperature several days before using for the best taste.

- Wrap cabbages in newspaper and store them just above freezing.

- Let beans dry in their pods on the vines out in the garden, then shell and store them in jars.

- Store root crops where they've grown in the garden. Before the ground freezes, cover carrots, beets, parsnips, horseradish, and Jerusalem artichokes with straw or chopped leaves deep enough to keep the soil from freezing. Mark the bed with a stick so you can locate it if it is covered by snow (which further insulates the soil beneath). As needed, shovel away the snow, set aside the mulch, dig up a week's supply of the buried produce, then replace the mulch and snow.

- The traditional way of storing harvested carrots and beets in sand can be a rather tedious process; instead, put them in plastic bags. Make about a dozen holes in each bag for ventilation and keep them in a polystyrene box in a cool room or unheated garage.

- Apples and pears can be stored the same way as carrots and beets. The punctured plastic bags retain enough moisture to keep the apples firm yet not enough to encourage rotting.

- A box in a box is another good way to store carrots, beets, apples, and pears: Get two cardboard cartons, one larger than the other. Stuff baseball-size balls of newspaper loosely in the space between the two boxes. Fill the inner box with fruits or vegetables and store the insulated chest in an unheated garage, porch, or cellar.

89 Six Ways to Support Tomatoes

All tomato plants do better with some sort of support, no matter whether they keep growing all season (indeterminate) or top out at a mere three or four feet (determinate). Supports keep the vines off the ground, clean, and away from puddles and slugs. They help expose the leaves and the fruits to the sunlight and reduce garden space taken up by the tomato patch. Tomato supports are easily fashioned from various materials as outlined below.

HOW TO DO IT

- Staking: Seven- to ten-foot-long bamboo poles, saplings, or milled lumber stakes worked two feet into the ground will hold even up the most vigorous indeterminate tomato plants. Staking is simple and inexpensive, but it requires both tying and pruning each plant. Be sure the stakes are in place before you transplant the tomato seedlings. Tie the plants to the poles at intervals of 12 to 18 inches and pinch out sprouting suckers so that no more than three stems are growing upward. Cut one-inch-wide

Staking (left) tomatoes on sturdy bamboo poles or wooden stakes is simple and inexpensive, but it requires pruning plants to only a few upward-growing stems and tying them to the stakes. Tomato cages may be homemade from wire fencing (right) or store-bought and are easy to install over seedlings, which need only occasional tucking in as they grow upward.

rings from panty hose legs and snip them open to make ribbons (they're soft and just the right length) for tying the tomatoes to the poles (see Tip #99).

• Caging: Millions of gardeners buy wire cages to support their tomato plants. These prefab cages are easy to install, and little or no pruning is required. Plants may require the occasional "threading"—directing stray stems back inside the cage—but this is a chore that takes only a few seconds. Store-bought tomato cages, tomato spirals, or tomato pens (square wire cages) are fine for determinate tomatoes, but even the tallest cages are too short for indeterminate varieties. For these, it is best to create

cages from wire mesh (six-inch-square gauge is best because you can reach through to pick the ripe fruits): Roll a length of the five-foot-wide mesh into a cylinder to make a cage 18 to 24 inches in diameter.

• Propping: Horizontal tomato support takes up more space than staking or caging but is particularly useful in windy regions and works especially well for shorter determinate tomatoes like 'Roma'. Laid horizontally and secured to the ground with stakes, the wire cylinders described above work well as props. Another easy way to prop tomatoes is to make a sturdy miniature "Quonset" from four-foot-wide concrete-reinforcing mesh. Have the wire mesh cut to whatever length

Propping plants horizontally (top) is particularly effective in windy regions and with short, determinate tomatoes. Covered with plastic, they can act as temporary greenhouses when the plants are small. Trellises (bottom) are space-efficient supports for growing tomatoes upward rather than outward.

you need—enough to cover two plants or an entire row—and arch it over the new transplants. Covered with plastic, these supports can double as a greenhouse while the plants are small. As the plants grow up and through the wire, the ripening fruit is kept up off the ground and stays clean and disease free.

• Trellising: For an instant tomato trellis, fix a section of heavy-gauge six-inch-square mesh wire between two sturdy, well-anchored posts (the opti-

mal height depends on the tomato variety you are growing). Set tomato plants at 18-inch intervals, and install support posts between every two plants. Every few days, weave the young vines back and forth through the grid, taking care to remove most or all suckers. If your plants outdistance the trellis, train them to grow horizontally rather than vertically.

• Weaving: Begin the basket-weaving support system as you would the trellis, placing anchor posts at each end

Weaving string between stakes to support tomatoes as they grow (top) works like a trellis; suckers should be pinched out to encourage vertical growth on a few stems. Tomatoes pruned to a single stem may also be supported with vertically strung twine suspended from an overhead wire (bottom).

of the tomato row, then driving additional stakes at 36-inch intervals (or two plants). Once the plants—pruned to two stems—are 14 inches tall, run a line of heavy-duty natural-fiber twine a foot from the ground down the row, securing it to each post as you go. When you reach the end of the row, fasten the line and head back up the row, "enclosing" the plants between the twine. Add new strands upward at eight-inch intervals as the plants grow.

• Stringing: Between two sturdy posts installed at either end of the row, stretch a heavy wire about a foot taller than the ultimate height of your tomato plants. Space the transplants about 18 inches apart, each next to a short garden stake pounded into the soil. Firmly tie one end of a length of garden twine to the stake at the foot of each plant; then knot the other end of the twine around the overhead support. Twine the growing plants up the strings, regularly removing suckers to

Determinate or Indeterminate? What's the Difference?

Determinate tomato plants top out at two to four feet, depending on the variety. Perfect for small gardens, a few popular cultivars in this group are 'Tiny Tim', 'Patio', and 'Roma'. With indeterminate tomatoes the sky is the limit. Given some sort of support they will keep growing upward until killed by frost. Most heirlooms, such as 'Brandywine', 'Mortgage Lifter', and 'Big Rainbow', are indeterminate tomatoes, as are popular hybrids like 'Big Boy' and 'Sunray'.

keep plants to a single stem. Every week, as the plants grow taller, gently guide the central stem around the twine, allowing at least one wrap for each flower cluster.

90 Ripening Tomatoes Indoors in Fall

Tomatoes are a top priority in many gardens. By growing plans with various fruit sizes and maturity times, you can enjoy tasty tomatoes all summer

long. In many regions, by mid-autumn the vines are still heavy with fruit, some red but many still green, even as frost threatens to nip the garden. It's time to pick all those unripe tomatoes and ripen them indoors. Tomatoes ripened indoors will not be as flavorful as those ripened in the garden, but their flavor will still be far superior to any tomatoes available in stores during the winter.

HOW TO DO IT

• Start picking surplus tomatoes as soon as the trees begin to show fall color. It's easiest to pull up entire tomato plants with the fruits still attached. Handle the plants gently to avoid dislodging the fruits. Hang the plants upside down by the roots in a cool but frost-free area.

• If you prefer, you can also pick the tomatoes off the vines, take them indoors, and spread them out on a table to slowly ripen. The warmer the storage area, the sooner the tomatoes will ripen.

Entire tomato plants can be pulled up at season's end and hung by their roots and sheltered from frost until the fruits ripen.

91 What to Do With a Bumper Crop

Just before the first frost, home gardeners with limited storage space must often rack their brains to find ways to deal with a bounty of ripening tomatoes, peppers, squashes, and eggplants. Rather than let this surplus go to waste, you can make a versatile end-of-the-season base for soup, sauce, or juice, perfect for using immediately or freezing for savoring during the winter.

HOW TO DO IT

• Skin, seed, and coarsely chop the tomatoes, put them in a large stockpot with a couple of cups of water, and simmer over low heat. Add some chopped onions, summer squash, eggplants, a green pepper or two, and whatever herbs are available and compatible, especially basil and parsley. Add salt, black pepper, and garlic to taste. Cook until the liquid is reduced to half the original volume. Cool the mixture and pour into pint- or quart-size containers suitable for freezing.

• Used as is or pureed with a little cream, the cooked medley makes a flavorful soup.

• For a more sustaining vegetable stew, add beans and short pasta as well as other vegetables like potatoes, corn, peas, and celery.

• To make an easy pasta sauce, add some chopped celery and carrots sautéed with bacon, ground beef, or sausage and little fresh or dried oregano.

• Puree the medley and serve cold or at room temperature as a delicious, vitamin-packed breakfast drink.

92 Vertical Vegetable Gardening

Gardens are limited in size horizontally, but they can grow skyward as high as support structures like poles, netting, and wire cages let them. Not all vegetables lend themselves to vertical growth, but ones with twining stems, like pole beans, or tendrils that curl around any nearby rigid object, like cucumbers, melons, winter squashes, pumpkins, and peas (both conventional varieties and sugar snaps) are naturals. In addition to taking up less space than those sprawling over the ground, vegetables grown vertically ripen sooner, are easier to pick, and stay cleaner.

HOW TO DO IT

• The twining, curling stems of pole beans can easily grow to 20 or 30 feet given a support that high. Unless you're interested in harvesting with a stepladder, however, keep the supports within reach.

• Many indeterminate varieties of tomatoes easily grow to six feet or more and should be supported (see Tip #99).

• Eggplants and peppers when laden with fruit can become top heavy and droop; to keep them vertical, encircle young plants with a wire cage and gently support the branches on the wires as they fruit.

To get the most from your garden space and keep tomatoes, beans, and cucumbers clean, healthy, and easy to pick, use vertical supports like cages and trellises fashioned from wire, string, and bamboo.

- Look around your yard and shed for homemade supports: Sugar snap peas, tomatoes, cucumbers, and pole beans will grow on a variety of readily available materials: Use saplings and pruned branches for beans and saplings with baling twine for sugar snaps; cages made from wire fencing support tomatoes; and even an old storm sash covered with wire will keep cucumbers up off the soil.

- Small pumpkins and melons can be grown vertically on trellises, but they might need slings for support should their weight be too great for their fragile tendrils (old panty hose work well for this; see Tip #99).

- See Tips #18, #87, and #89 for more support structures.

Trash to Treasure

93 Compost Bins Made of Reused Materials

Cement building blocks and discarded shipping pallets are handy materials for rigging up simple compost bins.

HOW TO DO IT

• Pick a site, preferably one that's level, gets some sun, and is out of the way yet conveniently located for frequent trips from the kitchen all year long.

• For a three-sided cement-block composter, build an enclosure that's five to seven blocks high along the back. To add stability, layer the blocks so that they overlap somewhat. Layer the blocks on the sides in progressively lower steps, tapering down to one block in front.

• To make a compost bin from shipping pallets, choose four sturdy pallets, stand them upright, and wire them together at the corners. For

extra ventilation at the bottom, place another pallet on the ground and arrange the standing pallets around it. Pallets are often available free at building-supply stores.

• If you build a double-wide enclosure and divide it into two sections, you can fill one half first and let it "cook"

This two-bin composting system, built from wooden pallets, has one bin full and cooking; the other is designated for adding fresh material.

A golf bag and cart get a new lease on life as a garden tote for long-handled tools and supplies.

while you continue to add compostable materials to the other bin (see Tip #26). In a few short months you will have finished compost ready for use in your garden. By then, the other bin should be ready to cook.

94 Golf-Bag Tool Carrier

A golf bag mounted on its two-wheeled pull cart makes a great garden-tool carrier. If you don't already have one moldering away in your basement or garage, a few visits to Saturday-morn-

ing tag sales will soon turn one up for very little money. Now all you have to do is find a new use for those clubs!

HOW TO DO IT

- Haul long-handled tools like your hoe, shovel, rake, and pitchfork in the club holder.

- The golf bag's various pockets designed for storing balls and golf accessories work great for hand pruners, seeds, gloves, twine, penknives, and other small gardening necessities.

Painted Tool Handles

As garden tools acquire a patina of age, the wooden handles become the same gray, brown, or tan color as most garden soils, making them easy to lose. Painting the tools bright orange gives them instant visibility. Brilliant yellow is even more noticeable. Another bonus of brightly painted tool handles: When they are borrowed by a neighbor, there is no question as to who owns what.

After they've served their purpose as place cards, herbs in rustic "pots" can be taken home by guests.

• The pull handle is handy for hanging a watering can and plastic bucket.

95 Herbal Place Cards

At family gatherings and dinner parties with friends and neighbors, confusion is minimized when guests are assigned a given place at the table. You can do it visually with place or name cards. Especially appropriate for a gathering of gardeners is a growing herb in a lithographed tin can or in a decorated plastic yogurt cup. Write the name of each guest on a plastic plant label (with the plant's name on the other side) and insert in the pot, with the guest's name facing the outside edge of the pot.

HOW TO DO IT

• Fill the bottom third of the container with fine gravel or pebbles; in the next third add a layer of sterile soil mix. Insert a rooted herb seedling—basil, parsley, sage, and rosemary are good choices—add more moistened mix, and gently tamp down and snug the mix around the plant. To assure that the young herbs are big enough to make a statement, start them a month or more before the dinner party. Pot them in the cans or predecorated yogurt cups a week before the party. Since there are no drainage holes in the herb "pots," water sparingly with an all-purpose liquid fertilizer at half strength.

• Use the place-card pots as favors. After the party, send your guests home with their potted herbs as a memento.

• Potted herbs make a unique and edible "floral" centerpiece on the dining-

A leaky garden hose can be converted to a sprinkler and moved wherever you need even, gentle watering; or camouflage it beneath a layer of mulch for use as a soaker hose.

room table. Encourage your guests to pinch off bits to enhance the flavor of their meal.

96 Homemade Soaker Hose

Annual borders, the vegetable garden, shrubs, trees, and perennials can be watered with a minimal amount of effort by snaking a homemade soaker hose through the beds. As water courses though the entire length of the hose, it spritzes out from dozens of tiny holes and slowly seeps into the ground.

HOW TO DO IT

- Get more mileage from a conventional garden hose that has sprung leaks by converting it into a soaker hose. Drill tiny holes along its entire length, cap the nozzle end, attach to a faucet, turn on the water, and you have a sprinkler that evenly and gently waters your plants.

- Soaker hoses can be permanently installed in the garden and hidden from sight by a layer of mulch, which also helps the soil retain precious moisture.

97 Mailbox Garden Storage

A place for everything and everything in its place. Gardeners can waste a lot of time looking for misplaced hand-tools—trowels, pruners, weeders, and the like. A handy place to stash them is

A rural-style mailbox installed on a fencepost in your garden can save time and effort by keeping small tools and supplies at hand.

in a watertight, metal rural-style mailbox somewhere in the garden.

HOW TO DO IT

• Use it to store small tools, wire, and seed packets, as well as spare eyeglasses, gloves, and of course, a hat. No more running back to the house or garage to fetch a trowel or some string—it's all right there in the garden mailbox. However, for your miniature storeroom to work, everything must be returned to the mailbox before you leave the garden!

98 New Lives for Clay Flowerpots

Most gardeners are frugal and tend to accumulate clay flowerpots of all sizes,

A bean tepee made of clustered bamboo poles can be secured at the top with an inverted flowerpot.

even cracked ones. Here are some reasons to continue doing so.

HOW TO DO IT

• Early in the season, cover newly planted seedlings with inverted pots to protect them from killing frosts.

• For an instant vertical accent, use an upside-down flowerpot beneath another holding a not-too-tall plant to double its height (see Tip #49). The bottom pot can be less than perfect if hidden behind lower-growing plants.

• A good use for cracked and frost-broken pots is to break them up into small shards and use them on a garden path, after the fashion of the oyster-shell paths in Colonial Williamsburg.

Inspired by the crushed-oyster-shell paths of Colonial Williamsburg, this shard path makes good use of frost-broken red clay flowerpots.

you can do the same thing with poinsettias. Buying several smaller plants is less expensive than one big, multi-branched poinsettia.

- To make a toad habitat for your garden, invert a clay pot with a large chip in the lip in a moist, shady spot. Make sure the chip creates a large enough "door" to accommodate a nice fat specimen of these beneficial garden creatures.

99 Panty Hose "Rope"

Soft yet strong, panty hose legs can be used as plant ties and as airy, quick-drying slings for heavy trellised vegetables like melons. Cut the legs into inch-wide strips to use instead of rope or twine. These sturdy nylon circles can be linked to make a rope chain much stronger and longer lasting than twine.

HOW TO DO IT

- Use the cut circles to tie tomatoes and dahlias to stakes—the wide strips won't cut into the stems.

- An eight- to ten-inch-wide strip of nylon hose will stretch to cradle a small pumpkin or melon growing on a vertical support (see Tip #92).

100 Reusing Toy Wagons

As your kids outgrow their childhood toys, don't be too hasty to get rid of

- A clay pot inverted over the top of gathered-together bamboo poles will hold a bean tepee together.

- To make a strawberry tower, choose three or four pots graduated in size and fill them with rich compost. Stack them one atop the other from large to small and plant them with strawberries. This construction also works beautifully with trailing petunias.

- If you like "yard art," fashion a flowerpot man relaxing in his garden. The pots for his head, arms, and legs are held together with thin rope threaded through the drainage holes.

- During the winter, most supermarket flower shops sell three-inch pots of daffodils and tulips already in flower. Nestle a bunch of them into a large clay pot to make one big, impressive container planting. Around Christmas

A child's pull wagon is a dandy carrier for getting your late-summer bounty from the garden to the house as well as for hauling bulky materials such as compost and paving stones.

those playthings—especially the four-wheeled pull wagon. Converting that Radio Flyer from a toy to garden use not only gives new utility to the wagon but can save your back from injury. Wagons with removable wooden sides can carry more than the low-sided ones, but plain steel ones are sturdier.

HOW TO DO IT

• The low center of gravity of a child's wagon makes it great for hauling heavy, bulky materials such as bales of straw or peat moss, fertilizer, cement, bricks—anything that's cumbersome.

Unlike wheelbarrows, which easily overturn when loaded, four-wheeled wagons are virtually untippable.

• Toward the fall when vegetable gardens are burgeoning, use your little wagon for hauling harvested produce from the garden back to the house.

• Use a toy wagon as a portable display for flowers—fill it with potted plants and wheel it to wherever you'd like some instant color.

Index and Contributors

Walter Chandoha has been a professional freelance photographer and writer for over 40 years, specializing in flora and fauna of the world. Much of his inspiration is drawn from his 46-acre farm in northwestern New Jersey, where he has many experimental gardens of flowers, vegetables, fruits, herbs, and ornamental grasses. His photographs and articles have appeared in books for Time/Life, Ortho, National Home Gardening Club, and Meredith Books, as well as in periodicals such as *Good Housekeeping, National Geographic, Country Living, House Beautiful, Architectural Digest, Organic Gardening, Garden Design, Better Homes and Gardens,* and *The New York Times.*

Illustrations Steve Buchanan

Photos Walter Chandoha

Special thanks go to the following Brooklyn Botanic Garden staff for reviewing the manuscript and contributing their ideas to the project: Jackie Fazio, director of horti-culture; Ellen Kirby, director Brooklyn GreenBridge, BBG's community horticulture program; and Anne O'Neill, curator of the Cranford Rose Garden.

More Information on Gardening

Designing an Herb Garden has everything you need to create a dazzling garden that's ornamental, practical, and fragrant, including simple plans, plant recommendations, and indispensable cultivation advice.

In *Annuals for Every Garden,* you'll find the plants that are just right for designing a spectacular ever-changing annual border, a display of drought-resistant flowers, an evening garden, and more, along with seed-starting and growing tips.

Ordering Books From Brooklyn Botanic Garden

World renowned for pioneering gardening information, Brooklyn Botanic Garden's award-winning guides provide practical advice for gardeners in every region of North America.

Join Brooklyn Botanic Garden as an annual Subscriber Member and receive three gardening handbooks, delivered directly to you, each year. Other benefits include free admission to many public gardens across the country, plus three issues of *Plants & Gardens News, Members News,* and our guide to courses and public programs.

For additional information on Brooklyn Botanic Garden, including other membership packages, call 718-623-7210 or visit our website at www.bbg.org. To order other fine titles published by BBG, call 718-623-7286 or shop in our online store at www.bbg.org/gardengiftshop.